End Page: The Bunga Raya (Hibiscus Rosa Sinesis) is Malaysia's national flower. This species has many colours but the one selected as the national flower is red and has five petals. This Bunga Raya batik fabric is designed by Batek Malaysia Bhd.

Cover: This gigantic granite rock is located in Low's Gully, Mount Kinabalu, Sabah.

MALAYSIA
WONDERS AND CONTRASTS

Published by

The five guiding principles of the Nation known as the Rukunegara have been formulated to bring about national unity to the multi-racial people of Malaysia.

- *Belief in God*
- *Loyalty to King and Country*
- *Upholding the Constitution*
- *Rule of Law*
- *Good Behaviour and Morality*

To God be the glory for all that He has done.

Chief Editor	:	Wong Swee Fook
Writers	:	Kit Lin
		Teo Ee Sim
Design	:	Foto Technik Sdn Bhd
Colour Separation	:	Sixty-Six Lithographic (Pte) Ltd
		Singapore
Printing	:	Tien Wah Press (Pte) Ltd
		Singapore

© Copyright Peter Chay 1986

All rights reserved. No part of this publication may be reproduced, stored in a retrieval system or transmitted, in any form or by any means, electronic mechanical, photocopying, recording or otherwise, without the written permission of Foto Technik Sdn Bhd and the copyright owner.

Perpustakaan Negara Malaysia

Cataloguing-in-Publication-Data

Malaysia – Wonders and Contrasts

ISBN 967-9981-04-5
1. Malaysia – Description and Travel
2. Malaysia – History
3. Malaysia – Social conditions
   915.95

Published by
FOTO TECHNIK SDN BHD, No: 116-A, Jalan Burhanuddin Helmi, Taman Tun Dr Ismail, 60000 Kuala Lumpur, Malaysia.
P.O. Box No: 11628. Cable: "AERIALFOTO PETALINGJAYA"

Aerial photographs taken with permission from the Director of National Mapping Malaysia.
DPNM. Sulit 10.11.3/Jld. 18/266

First Edition published 1986.
01038610

Much has been written and said about Malaysia, but there is not a single publication, film or tale that can, by itself, illustrate the soul of this colourful land. Appreciating the near impossibility of this task, this book will touch only a few of Malaysia's many facets.

Malaysia has long been the melting pot of Asia, a product of evolution brought about by the interaction of her three major races, and the influence of the modern West. The Malaysia of today is a country that carefully adopts modern values, yet comfortably retains her natural charm. This book could well be a most enjoyable "encounter" with Malaysia.

We wish to congratulate the publisher for its efforts, and the other co-sponsor for its support.

HAMZAH ABDUL MAJID
Director-General
Tourist Development Corporation
Malaysia.

MAS is proud to be a co-sponsor of this exciting new publication "Malaysia – Wonders and Contrasts". This is the second time that MAS has been involved in a similar project to help promote Malaysia.

The title of the book may suggest an overstatement on the country but anyone who knows Malaysia will acknowledge that with so much to offer it is difficult for any publication to oversell Malaysia. In fact I would venture to add that not enough has been written and portrayed of the country. As such this mammoth effort by the author is most timely.

I am confident that "Malaysia – Wonders and Contrasts" will not only create awareness of Malaysia but with the publication of a collection of rare aerial photographs, this publication will do justification to at least one aspect of Malaysia's rich heritage – the beauty of its natural environment.

DATO' ABDUL AZIZ ABDUL RAHMAN
Managing Director
Malaysian Airline System
Malaysia

The publisher would like to thank the Tourist Development Corporation and Malaysian Airline System which co-sponsored the publication of this book.

Acknowledgements

Many things are impossible to man, but to God all things are possible. Since its conception about three years ago, the publication of this pictorial volume on Malaysia has been beset by numerous obstacles and constant changes in format and theme, resulting in the project being shelved on many occasions. However, by God's grace, this project has finally become a reality.

I would like to thank the following for their invaluable support in helping to establish this project:

Tourist Development Corporation (TDC)
Malaysian Airline System (MAS)
Directorate of National Mapping
National Archives of Malaysia
National Museum
West Pacific Associates Pte Ltd
YB Justice Dato Mahadev Shanker
Daisy & Redzuan Kushairi
Mr & Mrs Kwa Inn Hock
Mr & Mrs Wu Ji Liow
Ms Kiang Teck Chin
Mr Wong Sai Fong
Ms Vialyne Low
Ms Amy Ooi

I would also like to express my heartfelt gratitude to my staff and those who had contributed to this project in one way or another.

Photo Credits

National Museum: 5, 100, 173, 177, 234, 239
Malaysian Airline System: 25, 54, 55, 186, 187, 188, 189, 190, 191, 192
Tourist Development Corporation: 170
Rubber Research Institute: 69
Johore Safari World: 116, 117
Yuen Kok Leng: 236
S. Sreedharan: 156, 157, 167, 171, 172, 174, 175, 176, 178, 179, 180, 196, 197
Stanley Loo: 36, 123, 127, 158
Lena Chan: 193
Cpt. Wong Yuen Fatt: 195, 198, 199
Janet Pan Ayun: 231, 235, 238, 240, 241, 242

CONTENTS

CHAPTER 1
Past heritage, present legacy   9

CHAPTER 2
Picturesque Malaysia   17

PERLIS	21
KEDAH	23
PULAU PINANG	33
PERAK	55
SELANGOR DARUL EHSAN	81
NEGERI SEMBILAN	117
MELAKA	127
JOHOR	155
PAHANG DARUL MAKMUR	165
TERENGGANU	199
KELANTAN	209
SARAWAK	221
SABAH	237

CHAPTER 3
**Kuala Lumpur —
minarets of old, visions of new**   251

Tunku Abdul Rahman Putra Al-Haj, Malaysia's first Prime Minister from 1957 to 1970. The Tunku is fondly referred to as Bapa Malaysia or Father of Malaysia.

CHAPTER 1

Past heritage, present legacy

Malaysia is a tropical wonderland situated in the heart of South-East Asia. Geographically, she is divided into two distinct regions, namely, Peninsular Malaysia extending from the Thai border to Singapore and separated by the South China Sea, Sabah and Sarawak on the north-west of Borneo Island. Her thirteen states and two Federal Territories cover a total area of about 330,000 square kilometres.

For the first-time visitors to Malaysia, the cliched expression that in the country, East meets West, takes on a new meaning. Malaysia's heritage is almost as old but extant as the Mesolithic relics unearthed in cavesites, now preserved in museums. Today, her existing infrastructure, social, economic, religious and political developments, environmental adaptations and ways of life are legacies of a tapestried past.

The written history of Malaysia began with the founding of the Malaccan Sultanate by a Sumatran prince, Parameswara. He had fled from his homeland first to Temasik (the present day Singapore) and then to the Malay Peninsula (now Peninsular Malaysia) to escape the Javanese onslaught. One day in 1403 while resting under a Malacca tree, he saw a bizarre occurrence whereby a ferocious hound was kicked by a mousedeer. Taking this to be a good omen, he decided to build a settlement and called it Malacca (Melaka) after the name of the tree under which he rested.

Malacca within the next decade of Parameswara's rule became a well-known seaport and trade centre in its own right, pioneering the beginning of the Malay Peninsula's entrepot trade. Merchants from all over flocked to Malacca to trade in perfume and spices. By the second decade of the fifteenth century, Malacca was already a flourishing trade centre, attracting traders from India, China, Arabia and Indonesia. Islam was propagated in the town by Muslim traders and during this century, Malacca embraced the religion, this move being later followed by other Malay states. To this day, Islam remains Malaysia's official religion and Islamic influence can be traced in the Jawi script of the Malay language.

The Indian merchants who arrived in Malacca built Hindu and Buddhist temples about the land and their ruins can still be found today in various states. Some local residents adopted the Hindu and Buddhist religions and Indian culture became integrated with local customs and rites. Even in the existing Bahasa Malaysia vocabulary, traces of Sanskrit can still be found.

The fifteenth century saw the dawning of Portugal's Age of Discovery. Malacca by this time was opened to European merchant ships, particularly those belonging to the Portuguese, Dutch and English. In 1511, Malacca fell into the hands of the Portuguese under the leadership of Alfonso de Albuquerque. The Portuguese proceeded to erect administrative buildings, churches, and fortresses. Under their rule, Catholicism found a niche in the hearts of some local residents. To promote further integration, the Portuguese authority encouraged intermarriages between their people and the local residents. Today, the descendants of Portuguese Eurasians can still be found in Malaysia, especially in the Portuguese Settlement in Malacca where many of them are fishermen.

The Dutch put an end to 130 years of Portuguese occupation of Malacca when they captured the settlement in 1641. Trading between the Malays and European merchants gradually extended to the states of Perak and Johore. The Dutch emulated their predecessors and constructed cathedrals and a number of buildings in Malacca. Some of these are still in existence in twentieth century Malacca; for instance, the Christ Church and Stadthuys which now form distinct landmarks in the heart of Malacca town.

By the eighteenth century, the English merchants of the British East India Company under the charter of Queen Elizabeth, took an increasing interest in Malacca as their ships docked at its harbour to be replenished with supplies before continuing their voyages to China. When the Sultan of Kedah permitted Britain to establish a settlement in Penang (Pulau Pinang), the British led by Captain

Francis Light, landed on the island in 1786 and this marked the year in which the Union Jack was first hoisted on Malayan soil. Under British guidance, changes were brought to the island and British laws were introduced for the first time.

Meanwhile, Europe was plunged into a turmoil with the advent of the French Revolution. With France threatening to take control of Dutch naval bases at the height of political unrest in the Netherlands, Malacca was transferred to the British in the late eighteenth century. In 1818, however, Malacca was returned to the Dutch only to be ceded to the British again six years later.

In 1819, the British took control of Singapore when the Sultan of Johor ceded this southern Malay island to them. Sir Stamford Raffles successfully turned it into a trading post. Seven years later, Singapore amalgamated with Malacca and Penang to form the Straits Settlement. Over in the Borneo Island, British influence continued. Captain James Brooke founded the saga of the rule of the 'White Rajahs' in Sarawak while Sabah became a British colony in 1946 when the British North Borneo Chartered Company handed the state to the British Government.

The discovery of tin in the states of Perak and Selangor led to the immigration of miners from mainland China and merchants from the Straits Settlement and other countries. Trading in tin increased in importance but the stability of this lucrative industry became uncertain when war broke out among the states' chieftains. This culminated in the decline of the export of tin and fearful that the merchants who invested money in the tin mines would turn to another western country for aid if they did nothing to solve this intransigence, the British sent Governor Sir Andrew Clarke to intervene in the chieftains' affairs. Sir Clarke managed to settle the dispute in the two states when the chieftains agreed to accept British Residents in their states, who would act as advisers on administrative matters and governing procedures. The two appointments marked the beginning of the British Residential System in Malaya. This system was later extended to Negeri Sembilan and Pahang which subsequently amalgamated with Selangor and Perak in 1896 to form the Federated Malay States.

British influence subsequently extended to the other states. Under a treaty in 1909, the Siamese Government handed over Perlis, Kedah, Terengganu and Kelantan to the British. British advisers, whose powers were almost similar to those of the Residents, were appointed in the four Malay states. By 1914, total British control over the Malay states was complete when Johor finally accepted a British adviser. Johor together with Perlis, Kedah, Terengganu and Kelantan were subsequently known as the Unfederated Malay States. Thus, prior to the Second World War, Malaya consisted of the Straits Settlement, the Federated Malay States and the Unfederated Malay States.

Meanwhile, the export of tin was recording a boom as was the population of Malaya with the pouring in of more Chinese immigrants to the country. Under the British, Malaya's economy was heavily dependent on tin and rubber. Rubber, a Brazilian import, was first planted in London as an experiment. The seedlings were later shipped to Malaya and planted in a village known as Kuala Kangsar where they initiated a prosperous industry. As early as 1920, Malaya was producing over half the world's production of rubber. As a result, workers from India and Ceylon (Sri Lanka) were brought in to work in the rubber estates.

Tin and rubber brought valuable income to the country which was used in the building of roads, administrative and social amenities. Continual boom in these industries saw further immigration of people from China, India and Ceylon.

Malaya's impressive economic growth came to a temporary standstill when the country was overrun by Japanese troops during the Second World War. The Japanese Occupation of Malaya (1941–1945) lasting for about three years and eight months created greater political awareness amongst the people of Malaya. Anti-colonialist feelings grew and soon the people of Malaya, fired by the spirit of nationalism, started a full-scale movement to obtain independence from the British.

When the Japanese finally surrendered on August 15, 1945, British troops returned to Malaya. On October 10 the same year, the British Government announced the formation of the Malayan Union. Under the new Union constitution, a British Governor was given full powers over the land while the powers of the Malay Sultans were almost completely stripped off. This, of course, angered the Malays who immediately held public rallies and demonstrations to strongly oppose the Union.

After lengthy consultations with the people, the British agreed to replace the Malayan Union Constitution with a new one drafted for the Federation of Malaya on January 21, 1948. In the same year, a nation-wide Emergency was declared in the new Federation when the Communist Party of Malaya took up arms against the Government. In the ensuing years, many innocent people were killed while much property was destroyed. A prominent feature of the Emergency was the Briggs Resettlement Scheme where squatters, mostly Chinese in remote areas fringing the jungles, were resettled in hundreds of new villages set up by the Government. By doing so, the Government succeeded in cutting off the communists' food supply. Today, these new villages are still in existence and they form an integral part of the Malaysian scenario.

The early years after the Second World War saw a rise in nationalistic consciousness amongst the people of Malaya who were all eager and ready for self-rule. Realizing this latest political development and also their failure to suppress the communist threat by military means, the British Government decided to win over the "people's hearts and minds" by providing them with more opportunities and privileges. For instance, the British Government conducted the country's first election in 1955 with the intention of getting the people to be directly involved in the Government. In the elections, the Alliance coalition party comprising the United Malays National Organization (UMNO), the Malayan Chinese Association (MCA) and the Malayan Indian Congress (MIC) which represented the Malays, Chinese and Indians respectively, swept 51 out of the 52 seats contested. However, the new Alliance Government was more interested in obtaining independence and requested the British to begin negotiations for full autonomy.

In the same year, attempts were made to get the communist terrorists to surrender. A meeting at Baling was held between the Government led by Tunku Abdul Rahman and the communists, who were represented by Chin Peng and Rashid Mydin. However, talks failed and the communists returned to the jungles to continue their armed struggle against the Government. The Emergency was finally lifted in 1960 but the communists still continued with their futile struggle. Many of them have since returned to society while a large number has either been killed or captured by government security forces.

Meanwhile, from January 18 to February 6, 1956, a constitutional conference for Malaya's full autonomy was held in London between the British Government and a Malayan delegation led by Tunku Abdul Rahman. After lengthy negotiation, the British agreed to grant independence to the Federation of Malaya with effect from August 31, 1957. A new nation was finally born on the stroke of midnight on August 30, 1957, with the lowering of the Union Jack followed by the hoisting of the new Malayan flag for the first time. Tunku Abdul Rahman was made the first Prime Minister.

Six years later on September 16, 1963, Singapore, Sabah and Sarawak joined the Federation to form Malaysia. Her sovereignty was however challenged by Indonesia and the Philippines. The former openly declared confrontation with the Federation while the latter demanded that the British return Sabah to her. After lengthy diplomatic efforts by all parties con-

This one kupang gold coin, equivalent to one-eighth of a Spanish dollar, was used in Kelantan during the sixteenth century. This ancient coin, which is believed to have originated from India, is also known as a kijang coin because one side has the motif of a kijang or barking deer. According to an old Malay animistic belief, gold had a spirit in the form of a kijang. The motif of the kijang, a solitary animal which occasionally gives out a loud cry, is now the logo of Bank Negara, Malaysia's Central Bank.

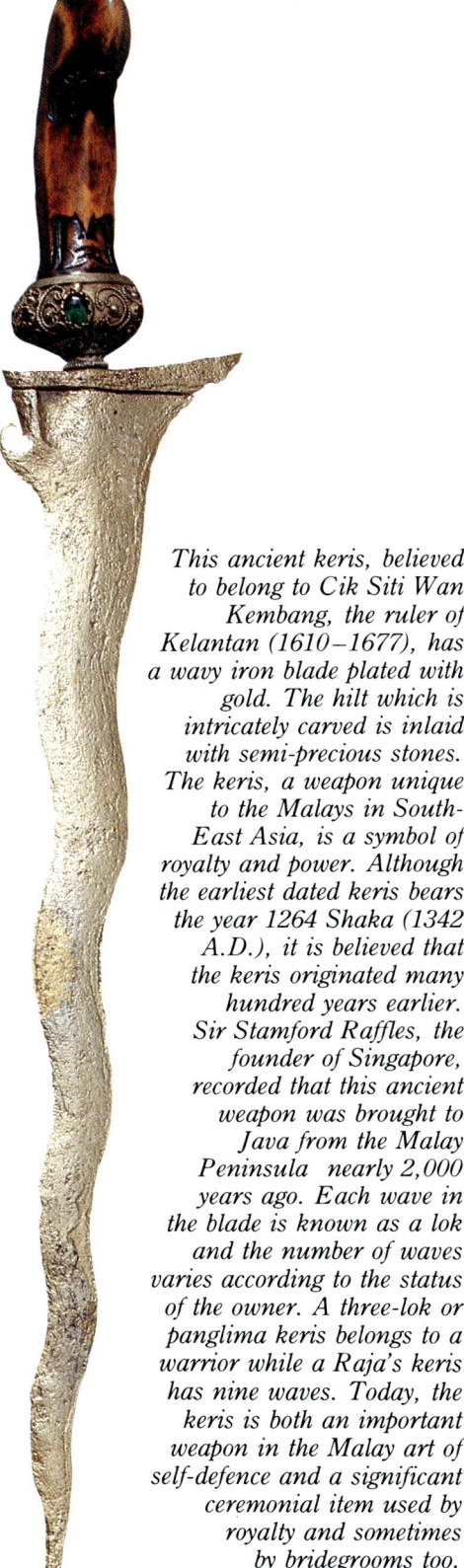

This ancient keris, believed to belong to Cik Siti Wan Kembang, the ruler of Kelantan (1610–1677), has a wavy iron blade plated with gold. The hilt which is intricately carved is inlaid with semi-precious stones. The keris, a weapon unique to the Malays in South-East Asia, is a symbol of royalty and power. Although the earliest dated keris bears the year 1264 Shaka (1342 A.D.), it is believed that the keris originated many hundred years earlier. Sir Stamford Raffles, the founder of Singapore, recorded that this ancient weapon was brought to Java from the Malay Peninsula nearly 2,000 years ago. Each wave in the blade is known as a lok and the number of waves varies according to the status of the owner. A three-lok or panglima keris belongs to a warrior while a Raja's keris has nine waves. Today, the keris is both an important weapon in the Malay art of self-defence and a significant ceremonial item used by royalty and sometimes by bridegrooms too.

cerned, these sudden developments were later amicably settled. However, on August 9, 1965, Singapore seceded from the Federation to become an independent republic.

In the ensuing years after her formation, Malaysia grew rapidly in all directions. One prominent feature of this growth is her economy which has diversified considerably to include other lucrative commodities such as palm oil, petroleum and natural gas and also manufacturing activities including the production of her own car, the Proton Saga.

An important factor that has contributed significantly to Malaysia's rapid development is the country's political stability. Malaysia is a democratic country ruled by a parliamentary system of government with a constitutional monarch. Parliament comprises the Yang di-Pertuan Agong or the King, who is the Supreme Head of State, and two Houses – the House of Representatives which is fully elected and the Senate which is partly elected and partly appointed. The Malaysian monarchy system is unique in that the King is elected from among the nine hereditary Rulers of the states of Perlis, Kedah, Perak, Selangor, Negeri Sembilan, Johor, Pahang, Terengganu and Kelantan at a Rulers' Conference. His term of office is five years and he can be removed from office by his fellow Rulers. As a constitutional monarch, the King's jurisdiction extends to the whole Federation. He is also the head of Islam of Pulau Pinang, Melaka, Sabah and the Federal Territories of Kuala Lumpur and Labuan all of which do not have hereditary Rulers. The hereditary Rulers are known as Sultans in all States except Perlis, where he is known as the Raja, and Negeri Sembilan, where he is called the Yang Di-Pertuan Besar.

The series of events and people involved in shaping Malaysia's spectral history have left behind a legacy that extends beyond those of a unique constitutional monarchy, ancient European citadels, Portuguese and Dutch baroque architecture, Eastern temples and shrines, and huge colonial buildings.

Today, tin and rubber still contribute to Malaysia's favourable balance of payments even though in recent years, their importance has declined considerably. Other important sources of income are petroleum, timber, palm oil, coconut products, pineapples, cocoa, pepper, tea and manufactured goods.

Malaysia has a plural society, her composition in Peninsular Malaysia being 56% Malays, 33% Chinese, 10% Indians and 1% *orang asli* and other mixed races. Sabah's population comprises 85% Bumiputra and others, and 15% Chinese. In Sarawak, 71% are Bumiputra and others, while 29% are Chinese. This ethnic diversity is matched by the wide range of lifestyles and cultures within her society.

Although the various ethnic groups are united under the nametag "Malaysians", they still maintain their individual lifestyles, which are determined by and reflect their differing cultural heritage. No two ceremonial rites are the same, although one may be influenced by another, as in the Baba-Nyonya (Straits-born Chinese) wedding ceremony which contains a number of Malay customs. The various groups celebrate their own festivals; the Malays celebrate Hari Raya Puasa, the Chinese, the Chinese New Year and the Indians, Deepavali. Each group has its own ways of greeting and carrying out a conversation, of dressing and eating. Each group also has its own lore and customs to be kept for posterity. Similarly, such diversity is also reflected in their songs, dances, poetry and other visual arts.

Malaysians are generally multi-lingual, the average person being tutored in at least two languages, the erudite at least three. Since Bahasa Malaysia was made the country's national language in an attempt to unite her multi-ethnic people, most Malaysians speak and write the language fairly well. Bahasa Malaysia is the medium of instruction in all national schools and institutions of higher learning. However, English is still widely used in many fields such as commerce and law. In many households, educational bodies and work-places, Bahasa Malaysia, English, Chinese, Tamil and other vernacular dialects are miscible in the tongues of the average Malaysians.

The Malaysian education system, which is modelled after the British system, provides the people with thirteen years of free education up to upper secondary school level (Form Six or "A" Level). To ensure that the country's manpower needs are met, the Government has also set up seven universities and a number of technical, vocational and polytechnic schools and colleges.

By the same token, Malaysia's present judicial system and courtroom procedures are akin to the British system of law. However, since the setting up of the Supreme Court on January 1, 1985, the country's judicial system has been fully independent.

Islam is Malaysia's official religion. However, religious tolerance guaranteed by the Constitution has allowed the people to embrace, adopt and practise other religions such as Buddhism, Taoism, Hinduism and Christianity. Part of Malaysia's mysticism is attributed to her many religious houses found in her thirteen states and two Federal Territories. Golden domes, minarets and cupolas monopolize grand views in city squares and the countryside; Melaka is the vanguard of Gothic cathedrals and Pulau Pinang's skyline is marked by a deluge of ornate Hindu shrines and opulent Buddhist temples.

Today, Malaysia is still undergoing rapid changes and modernization. Despite this, there is no doubt that as a nation, Malaysia's present identity rests in her vast stockpile of legacies bequeathed her by her kaleidoscopic past.

CHAPTER 2

Picturesque Malaysia

Colour is a basic ingredient in the appeal of Malaysia, from the intense deep green of the tropical plants, blue of the distant hills to the multi-coloured, rainbow-hued costumes of the people. After the shock of seeing primary colours so merrily juxtaposed has receded, the next fact that impinges on the senses is that Malaysia is not a one-facet, one-economy, one-people, country.

If anything, there are at least two sides to Malaysia: the rural and the urban; the agrarian and the industrial; the mountains and the lowlands; the traditional and the modern. There are four main groups of people in Peninsular Malaysia and 26 ethnic ones in Sabah, 25 in Sarawak.

Topographically, the mountain core dominates in Malaysia, thickly swathed in tropical rainforests which are believed to be among the oldest on earth. Too thick to penetrate in some cases, too high for the ordinary person to reach, these jungles have grown undisturbed for more than 130 million years.

While these jungles covering two-thirds of the country are uncharted territory, the fringes on Peninsular Malaysia support the *Orang Asli* or Original Man as the indigenous people are called. The main tribes – Negrito, Senoi and Jakun – eke out an existence that is barely subsistence. With their primitive weapons like blowpipes, crude spears, arrows and bamboo cages they trap animals for food. Some practise shifting agriculture, while others are permanent settlers, but however they supplement their food requirements it is the jungle that is their terrain.

Historians and anthropologists agree that they are descended from the Austroasiatic and Austronesian peoples of Southern Indo-China and China who filtered into the Malay archipelago and hinterland. Today, they remain largely unaffected by the urbanization that grips the rest of the country although some of them have begun to venture into the towns in search of bettering their lot socially and economically.

In Sabah and Sarawak – the fringe-jungle dwellers are tribespeople known as Ibans, Dayaks, Bajaus, Muruts and Kadazans with blood ties to many who now live in villages outside the jungles. The Ibans are the largest tribe in Sarawak and their communal "longhouses" sheltering many families, are a few stages removed from the rudimentary shacks of the *Orang Asli* in Peninsular Malaysia. It is these longhouses, the highly-developed riding skills of the Bajau horsemen, the cadences of the gentle Ibans, the festive lifestyles of the Dayaks in addition to the variety of customs, costumes and languages that provide some of that rich "colour" that is Malaysia.

Given that two-thirds of the country are still under jungle, Malaysia's timber resources are quite considerable. Large tracts are designated jungle reserves or protected as national parks although controlled logging in concessionary areas is allowed. Selective logging particularly for the desired tropical hardwoods like *ramin, cengal* and *balau* has helped the country earn valuable foreign exchange to the extent that it is now one of the largest ringgit earners.

Moving from the sparsely populated, densely covered jungle interior to the coastal lands, the contrast is immediately apparent. The north-western states of Kedah and Perlis in Peninsular Malaysia are agrarian, often dubbed the "rice bowl of Malaysia" because of the multitudinous hectares of paddy fields. Here, in the early hours of a dew-heavy morning, farmers can be seen in the countryside moving like shadow play figures, as they head for their fields. Through the noon-day sun until the light of evening begins to fail, the farmers lavish care and fertiliser to make the land produce.

Further south, the alluvial soils of Negeri Sembilan, Melaka and Johor have destined them for agriculture too. With government assistance in the form of land schemes, releasing and opening new land for the cultivation of diversified crops and backing these up with technology and irrigation systems, the farmers earn a decent living. Rubber is the main crop and grown either in small holdings in these land schemes or in huge, orderly estates that continue for many kilometres. Planted as they are in mesmeric rows along the countryside, the rubber trees rich with sap stand like sentinels. After the trees reach maturity, men and women tappers venture out in the morning mist to tap the trees. With a skilled surgeon's touch, they are careful to cut just deep enough to let the latex ooze yet not too deep as to damage the tree forever.

In recent years, as world demand for palm oil increased, vast estates of palm oil started burgeoning in these states. Its increasing importance is evident as the country seeks to broaden its traditional dependence on the twin pillars, tin and rubber. Other crops that are being emphasized include cocoa, coffee, pepper, pineapple, sugar cane and soya bean.

The industrial economy, the urban and the more modern sides to Malaysia occur in the lowlands with the states of Perak and Selangor, the acknowledged industrial leaders. Here where population density is highest, the discovery of tin had provided the impetus for their astonishing development. Although tin is found in nine out of eleven Peninsular Malaysian states in two main belts, the richer one is the western belt that runs along the flanks of the Main Range and bounding both sides of the secondary granite ranges to the west of the Main Range which just happens to fall in the Kinta Valley of Perak and Kelang Valley of Selangor. Despite the concentrated mining efforts over the years, it is estimated that there are still 763,000 cubic metres of tin lying in Malay Reservation land, waiting to be mined.

The history of the tin rush in these states is well documented, the written records painting a period of upheavals when feuds and clan clashes among tin miners in the 1800 s were commonplace. After the devastation of the Second World War and particularly in the post-Independence period, development in the two states accelerated at a tenfold pace. Commercial activities boomed as the urban centres ringed further and further out, while improved transport and communication systems, sanitation and housing aided the modernization thrust.

The Kelang Valley epitomizes the industrial and commercial pace in the country and exercises a strong magnetic pull on job-seekers from neighbouring states. The Federal Capital of Kuala Lumpur pulsates with the rhythms of any sophisticated, forward-thrusting global city. The high-speed whirrs of computers turn the wheels of banking, finance and large commercial enterprises while at nightfall, the beat of a different drum leads the pace – the syncopated, soul-stirring thumps of disco bands in the hotel clubs or new, highrise shopping plazas. Just outside the City limits, the suburbs of Petaling Jaya, towns like Shah Alam and Kelang are just as restless, as much hives of activity as the Federal Capital. For here are found the factories, the auto assembly plants, the Malaysian equivalent of Silicon Valley, complete with multinational participation turning out the fingernail-sized chips and other components for electronics-based products.

Pulau Pinang has its share of electronics plants and industries and at 1,000 persons per square kilometre is more densely populated than Perak and Selangor. But its chief allure for visitors is its fine beaches, followed very closely by its inimitable charm. With the recent completion of the Penang Bridge – the longest in Asia – the island will be even more closely linked to the rest of the country. Apart from the physical bridging of distances which would be highly convenient to businessmen and commuters, the Bridge is a technological and aesthetic triumph that even its detractors acknowledge.

Moving east across the Main Range, via the East-West and Karak Highways brings one to the east coast states of Kelantan, Terengganu and Pahang. Out of a total of 15.7 million Malaysians only 16% or 2.5 million live in these states, generally occupying themselves with fishing off the long coastline. In the months when the turbulent North-East Monsoon lets off, the carved and painted *perahu* (fishing craft) of these fisherfolk can be seen putting out to sea in the still-dark hours of dawn. The South China Sea is still yielding up nets of crabs, squids, lobsters, shrimp and fish of many varieties. When the craft return in the evening, the day's catch is unloaded, packed in ice and trucked to markets all over the peninsula, to canning factories and to bulk buyers. The East Coast fisherman survives on the quantity and quality of his catch, no matter how bountiful or meagre that may be. But his cultural and family lives are rich indeed – for here is the heartland where handicrafts like silver and brass-working, *mengkuang*-weaving, *batik*-printing, carving, traditional dance-dramas and unique past-times with giant kites and tops have no rival anywhere else in the peninsula. The fierce attachment to home and family life and to customs and traditions provides counterpoint to modern values, providing the country with a deeper sense of itself.

While a small percentage of people in the East Coast live and work in towns, the discovery of off-shore oil could bring about an increase in population and rapid development of the towns. As things stand, the pace does not look to be one that is rampantly unmanageable nor should it destroy the cultural fabric of the area.

The other half of Malaysia across the South China Sea is an elongated strip about 1,720 kilometres long and about 256 kilometres wide on the island of Borneo. Both the states of Sabah and Sarawak share similar physical features with Peninsular Malaysia in that the interior is mountainous and the most developed parts of the country are concentrated in the coastal areas. Nearly 80% of the two states are covered in rainforest and farming is confined to the outskirts of the coastal lands. Rivers often form the communication links between the interiors and the towns where roads are not in existence. In the towns proper – as in Kota Kinabalu, the Federal Territory of the port Labuan, the timber town of Sandakan in Sabah and the oil-rich towns of Miri and Bintulu in Sarawak – modern road systems and airways have been developed.

Because of the vast potential of these two states the low density population (15 persons per square kilometre in Sabah and 11 persons per square kilometre in Sarawak), the discovery of off-shore oil, the touristic attractions more natural than man-made, it could be that they will come into their own as the "land of opportunity" for Malaysians.

In the pages that follow, each State is individually explored, unravelling for the onlooker colours that seem more vibrant, contrasts that appear more pronounced than casual contact would reveal.

(previous page) A stretch of Pulau Langkawi's white sandy beaches.

CHAPTER 2
Picturesque Malaysia

PERLIS — The Smallest State

A true border state on the Malaysian-Thai border, Perlis at 795 square kilometres is the country's smallest state.

Its history dates back to the ancient Sultanate of Kedah when it was once part of this kingdom, but it became a separate state after the Siamese Occupation in 1721. In 1905, Perlis obtained from Thailand the services of a European adviser and financial aid to help in the administrative and financial affairs of the State. The adviser remained in the State until the signing of the Anglo-Siamese treaty in 1909 whereby Perlis came under British rule. During the Japanese Occupation Perlis was returned to Thailand who appointed a governor to take charge of the affairs of the State. Perlis again came under British sovereignty when the Japanese surrendered.

Like its next-door neighbour, Kedah, Perlis' agricultural wealth is counted by the stalks of paddy that grow on its flat lands. Much of this northern state is under paddy cultivation where farmers live in simple wooden houses, fanned by coconut and papaya trees. The villages are surrounded by paddy fields marked out in quadratic squares resembling a giant carpet rolling to the horizon.

In Perlis' countryside, men ploughing the paddy fields behind water buffaloes and women in conical hats planting seedlings is a typical scene although many of the farming activities are gradually being mechanized. During the harvesting month, the paddy is reaped and gleaned, and usually there is much feasting after the harvests particularly if the yields have been bountiful.

As in the villages, the rest of Perlis is only a little marred by modernism. There is still much natural beauty in the state such as Gua Kelam or "Dark Cave", a magnificent example of limestone formation located at the foothills of Kaki Bukit (which literally means foothills) near the Malaysian-Thai border. Countless grey-coloured stalactites and stalagmites adorn the ceiling and floor of the cave while the sides are smoothed by water droplets falling from the roof through the years. A wooden bridge running through this 600-metre cave links Kaki Bukit with the border village of Kampung Wang Klian. First used by Chinese tin miners (Kaki Bukit is one of the two places in the country where lode-mining is practised), the bridge now serves as a short cut for the residents of Kampung Wang Klian and Kaki Bukit.

Everywhere in Perlis, in the countryside and the capital town of Kangar, life goes on at a snail's pace for its people of close to 150,000. The only exception perhaps is Padang Besar on the north of Kangar. This busy and popular border outpost draws large crowds of shoppers every weekend. It is now being redeveloped to attract more shoppers from both sides of the border.

In the royal town of Arau, the Sultan's palace stands in regal repose. This splendid building is the home of the royal family and also the state's regalia. The Royal Mosque is also found in this peaceful, stately town. Kuala Perlis at the mouth of Sungei Perlis is the ferrying point for holiday – makers to Langkawi Island while nearby is located Bukit Kubu, a new recreational park.

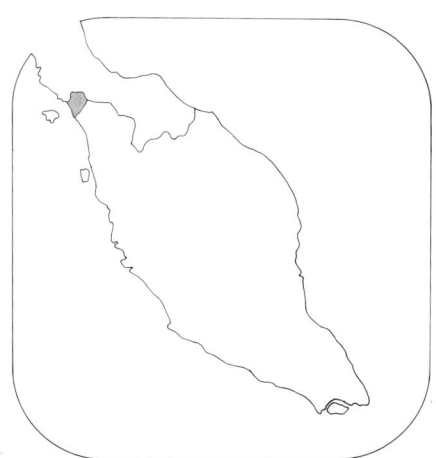

Kangar, the capital and administrative centre of Perlis. The surrounding rice plain is dotted with solitary limestone outcrops whose caves were believed to have been the homes of Stone Age men.

CHAPTER 2
Picturesque Malaysia

KEDAH — The Rice Bowl State

On a clear day soon after tender green paddy seedlings have been transplanted, the main trunk road to Kedah is often bounded on both sides by a green sea of these plants undulating kilometre after kilometre. In a few weeks more, the green changes to light golden stalks plump with the cereal that would end up in the rice bins of at least half the nation's households.

Little wonder then, that this 9,425 square kilometre state with its 1.2 million people is fondly dubbed the "Rice Bowl of Malaysia".

But Kedah's contribution extends beyond its agricultural bounty. It is one of the oldest states in Malaysia as evidenced by archaeological digs around the base of Kedah Peak. The evidence shows that at the beginning of the Christian era, Indian ships from South Asia sailed to Kedah and built a settlement at Bujang Valley near Sungei Petani. The ruins, first discovered in the nineteenth century, have since 1970 been identified and reconstructed by the Malaysian Museums Department. These "candi" or tomb-temples may eventually form the core of the national historical park, now under consideration. Another historical site is at Kuala Kedah where a Portuguese fort of the seventeenth century has left its mark.

Lying off the coast of Kedah is the Langkawi Island, a cluster of 99 islands where romantic legends combined with inviting white beaches have made it a popular beach resort. The largest island is Langkawi Island also known as the "Isle of Legends". The most famous legend is the tale of Mahsuri, a Malay princess much celebrated for her beauty, who was unjustly accused of adultery and in accordance with the laws of the land then, was sentenced to be executed. Mahsuri, however, proved her innocence upon her execution when she shed white blood. The islanders were in remorse over the wrongful execution but too late – the princess had placed the island under a curse for seven generations, during which time it was plagued by enemy attacks and natural disasters, among others. That was probably a long time ago in another era, for today the island is rapidly being transformed and an international resort project is being developed at Tanjung Rhu. Mahsuri's tomb stands in a village in this very island and serves as a reminder of the sad tale of this unfortunate princess.

Langkawi spells of many smaller legends. For instance, after Mahsuri's death, the island was invaded by foreigners. The islanders repudiated their enemies by burning their paddy fields. Today in Padang Masirat, or Field of Burnt Rice, 19 kilometres from the main town off Kuah, the charred remains of burnt rice still surface after a heavy rain. Then there is Pulau Dayang Bunting, or Island of the Pregnant Maiden, the second largest island in the Langkawi group. Found here is a fresh water lake known as the Tasik Dayang Bunting, and according to local folkfore, a couple childless for 19 years had a baby after drinking its water.

Many other things mystify and fascinate one about Pulau Langkawi. One of these is the Beach of Black Sand, and the mystery of its black sand has never been solved.

Mainland Kedah is not short of its own legends. Its capital, Alor Setar, is the home of the state's largest mosque, Masjid Zahir, the Balai Nobat, a traditional royal orchestra building and the Balai Besar or Great Hall. Legend has it that the Hall used to resound with drumbeats before the time of morning prayers. However, no one saw the drums or the drummers.

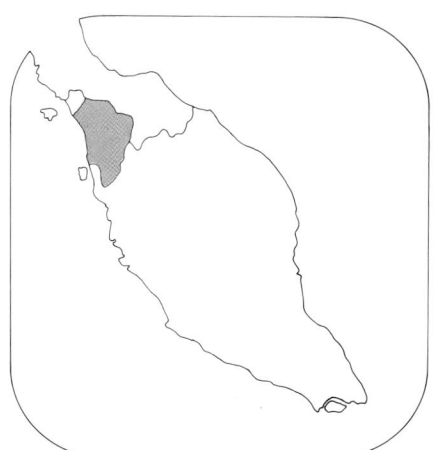

Under the Muda Irrigation Project, a dam on the upper reaches of the Muda River and a vast network of irrigation canals criss-crossing the Kedah Plain were constructed. This successful project together with the discovery of new paddy strains which can produce higher quality yield have resulted in a boon for local rice production in recent years.

5 Bujang Valley is the site of Malaysia's proposed national historical park. Located about 30 kilometres from Sungei Petani, the valley houses the ruins of a 350-square kilometre ancient Indian city discovered in the middle of the nineteenth century. Archaeological evidence reveals that Indian ships sailed from south Asia and arrived in Kedah about 1,000 years ago. The south Indian seafarers then set up a settlement in the valley. The existence of this ancient settlement was chronicled by the Chinese scholar I-Ching and Arab travellers in the seventh and fifteenth centuries. The ruins of numerous tomb-temples (*candi*) are scattered in the valley. Some of them have been identified and reconstructed by the Malaysian Museums Department since 1970. Artefacts, books and documents of the Bujang Valley are housed at the Bukit Batu Pahat Museum.

6 Kuala Kedah, a coastal fishing village at the mouth of Sungei Kedah is rich in historic past. Its inhabitants are mainly simple fisherfolk and paddy planters. Located here are the ruins of an old Portuguese fort built in the 1770s. It withstood a treacherous Siamese attack in 1821 for six days before it fell. Today, it has been partially restored.

7 *(following page)* Lying on this absolutely flat Kedah Plain is the state capital, Alor Setar. The magnificent Zahir Mosque and the Balai Besar (Great Hall) of unique Thai architecture built in 1898 are located near the padang. The Great Hall is used by His Royal Highness, the Sultan of Kedah on auspicious occasions. The Balai Nobat opposite the Great Hall houses the Kedah's traditional royal orchestra instruments (*nobat*). The *nobat* is considered an important part of the State's regalia – no Kedah Sultan is recognized as a legitimate ruler if he has not been installed to the accompaniment of the *nobat*.

8   9

8 Quietly reposed on the northern coast of the main Langkawi Island near the famous Tanjung Rhu beach is this peaceful fishing village.

9 Located near Kuah, Langkawi Island's main town, this 200-room Langkawi Island Resort commands a panoramic view of the sea.

10 *(following page)* One of Langkawi's most popular beaches is Tanjung Rhu (Cape of Casuarina) on the northern tip of the main island. A multi-billion dollar Langkawi Resort City Project is taking shape here. This intergrated resort complex will initially comprise five international hotels around a giant swimming pool, a water-sports complex, condominiums, townhouses and residential units. When fully completed before the end of 1990, it is expected to be South-East Asia's biggest resort complex. Located amongst the limestone cliffs in the distance is Gua Cerita (Story Cave), a legendary cave inscribed with ancient writings from the Holy Quran.

CHAPTER 2
Picturesque Malaysia

PULAU PINANG — The Pearl Of The Orient

Like the real, lustrous pearl it is compared to, Pulau Pinang has an allure that draws the explorer deeper and deeper, layer by layer. The 285 square kilometre island together with the sliver of 738 square kilometres on the mainland called Province Wellesley or Seberang Perai, constitute the state on which one million Malaysians live and work.

But it is Pulau Pinang itself, the island, which is particularly charming. And of all its attractions, none has been sung with more fervour than its beaches, fine enough to draw even world-weary travellers. Perhaps it is the romance in the names of these beaches that helps to perpetuate the island's infinite appeal. Who can fail to detect a faint, sweet scent of jasmine or frangipani when the name "Tanjung Bungah" or Cape Of Flowers is mentioned? Who but the cynical can forget Moonlight Bay on the night of a bright, full moon with only the whispering of casuarinas to break a dreamy silence? Or not hear the music of Titi Kerawang, that natural fresh water pool near Batu Ferringhi? Finally, the most sought-after strip of beach, Batu Ferringhi: smart, sophisticated, up-beat international hotels with a style and a host of facilities to make a holiday paradisial.

After giving in to the seductive beaches of Pulau Pinang, a foray made into its touristic sights will pay off handsomely. For starters, there is the Kek Lok Si Temple whose crowning touch is a Pagoda with 10,000 Buddhas. Then, the Snake Temple full of Wagler's Pit Vipers, coiled semi-comatose, subdued by the heady wisps of incense; the Thai Wat Chayamangkalaram with a 32.4 metre reclining statue of the Buddha; the Kuan Ying Ting Temple which is Pulau Pinang's oldest; the Kapitan Kling Mosque all domes and minarets; St. George's Church and the Cathedral of the Assumption, massively white and imposing.

Futher afield, a funicular railway sturdily hauls visitors up Penang Hill, a vantage point that reveals the spread of the town below. The Botanical Gardens occupying 30.4 hectares of greenery have a fine assortment of flora of Malaysia and other parts of the tropics. Here macaques, grown accustomed to humans, take nuts and bananas from visitors with no hint of shyness. Fort Cornwallis can be made out with a high powered binoculars. Built in 1808 to repel enemy attacks, it also marks the spot that Captain Francis Light first alighted on the island back in 1786 – making Pulau Pinang the oldest British settlement in Peninsular Malaysia. An amphitheatre and a museum are now sited in the fort, a promenade-like Esplanade nearby.

Once a year in December, a month-long festival is held on the island. Throng upon throng of visitors and locals alike cheer on the muscular rowers in their dragon boats, ogle the float processions, try their hand at angling, and gawk as daring men balance hefty, 13-metre high bamboo poles with huge colourful flags on the most unlikely places: head, shoulder, stomach, chin and forehead.

Such colour, such derring-do is probably only equalled by the plethora of food, glorious food available night and day in Pulau Pinang. In this "Pearl of the Orient", the variety of food is infinitely pleasing whether served at roadside stalls, hawker centres, restaurants or clubs.

With the opening of the Penang Bridge, one of the longest in the world, it is an open secret that the state will be galloping on to even greater development and prosperity.

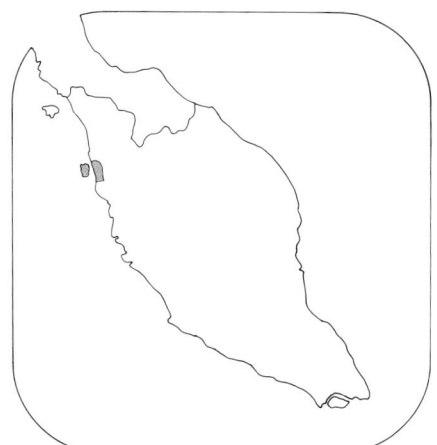

The Municipal Council building at the Esplanade is one of Pulau Pinang's most elegant landmarks. This palladian-style building was built at the end of the nineteenth century.

12 The Penang Bridge, one of the world's ten longest bridges, links mainland Peninsular Malaysia to Pulau Pinang. Completed in 1985, the 13.5-kilometre long bridge is designed to withstand any earthquake up to 7.5 on the Richter scale. The middle span of the bridge has a 225-metre vertical clearance to allow ships with a maximum mast-height of 30 metres to pass.

13 14
   15

13 Georgetown, the state capital and one of Malaysia's main ports. Towering above the city centre is the 65-storey Kompleks Tun Abdul Razak (Komtar), the tallest building in South-East Asia. Across the sea is Seberang Prai or Province Wellesley.

14 Bayan Lepas Airport.

15 The ferry terminal in Pulau Pinang is a concourse of people, vehicles and cargoes. With the newly-completed $850 million Penang Bridge, this ferry terminal is slowly losing its importance.

16 Arahant Upagutta Temple, one of the numerous Buddhist temples in Pulau Pinang.

17 St George's Church, one of Malaysia's oldest churches. It was built in 1818 by convict labour but was partly destroyed by Japanese bombs during the Second World War in December 1941. It stood roofless and unused for seven years before it was finally restored for public worship in July 1948. Based on European classical architecture adapted to suit the country's tropical climate, the well proportioned church has a lofty spire and white columns rising from a marble floor.

18 Pulau Pinang State Mosque. Opened in 1980, this magnificent mosque has a grand hall and a 50-metre high minaret. The ceiling of the hall is designed in the shape of a hibiscus, Malaysia's national flower.

19 The Lady Fatimah or Virgin Mary Monument to commemorate Mary's ascension. In the background is the Pulau Pinang State Museum and Art Gallery building. The museum houses some fine collections of historical items including historical paintings, photographs and documents from the time of Captain Francis Light to the Japanese surrender in 1945 and Chinese carvings and furniture. The gallery has many fine paintings and holds regular exhibitions by both local and foreign artists throughout the year.

20 *(following page)* The Kek Lok Si, Malaysia's largest Buddhist temple, is situated on the hill slopes of Ayer Itam. Built around 1890, this magnificent temple has a number of prayer halls housing many deities, a monastery, a library of Buddhist literature and the Pagoda of Ten Thousand Buddhas. The seven-tiered pagoda combines the art of three different cultures – the lower section is Chinese, the middle section Thai and the uppermost section Burmese in design. Further up the slopes is a giant statue of the Chinese deity, the Goddess of Mercy.

21, 22 The Snake Temple in Bayan Lepas is perhaps the only one of its kind in the world. Built in 1850 in dedication to the Chinese deity, Chor Soo Kong, this temple is the home of poisonous Waglers Pit Vipers. The snakes, semi-comatosed by the heady wisp of burning incense, coil around the legs of altar tables, joss sticks stands, incense pots and branches of potted plants. The snakes come from nearby areas and during the deity's birthday on the sixth day of the first Chinese Lunar Month, the number of snakes is said to increase considerably. Although venomous, the vipers remain docile and have never bitten anyone.

23 The Kapitan Kling Mosque, a typically Indian-influenced building in Leboh Pitt. Built in 1800 by Cauder Mohuddeen, who was then a wealthy *kapitan* (headman), this tranquil single-minareted mosque was first used by Pulau Pinang's Indian Muslim settlers.

24 Batu Ferringhi's famous beach is nicknamed "the Golden Row". Located along its stretch of white sandy beach are luxurious hotels such as the Golden Sands and Rasa Sayang hotels. The restaurants here serve a diversity of palatable cuisines that would titillate the most fastidious taste buds. The beach here is an ideal spot for swimming, aquatic sports or sun-bathing beneath the equatorial sun.

25
26

25 Dragon boat races off Gurney Drive are held during the Penang International Boat Festival in July and the month-long Pesta Pulau Pinang (Penang Festival) in December. Such races are rampant with the cheers and shouts of boisterous crowds as the competing teams row their boats furiously towards the finishing line. The vessels are known as dragon boats because of the skilfully-carved wooden "dragon heads' projecting from their bows.

26 The Eastern and Oriental Hotel or popularly known as the E & O Hotel. Started by the Sarkies Brothers, the famous Armenian hoteliers, in 1885, this hotel is one of the country's oldest.

27 *(following page)* Gurney Drive is a popular venue for food-lovers and evening strollers. There are numerous side-walk stalls and mobiled hawkers selling a variety of simple and yet delicious local delicacies.

28 Batu Maung, a fishing village on the south-eastern tip of Pulau Pinang. A shrine on a rocky promontory here marks the footprint of Admiral Cheng Ho, the "three-jewelled eunuch prince" of the Ming dynasty in China. It is believed that this footprint and another in Pulau Langkawi, an island about 110 kilometres north of Penang Island, are one pair belonging to the famous Ming admiral. According to villagers, whoever lights a joss-stick and places it in an urn beside the legendary footprint will receive good fortune. Located in some forested hills here is a maze of labyrinths, machinegun nests, ammunition dumps, bunkers and other concrete-steel relics of the Second World War.

29 The Guillemard Reservoir is one of Pulau Pinang's main catchment areas providing water supply to scores of homes and industries on the north-eastern part of the island.

30 Bukit Bendera or Penang Hill is a group of hills on the north of Pulau Pinang. Located about 830 metres above sea level is West Peak, Pulau Pinang's highest point. Penang Hill is a popular hill resort with a hotel, some holiday bungalows, a tea kiosk serving snacks and drinks, a police station, a post office, gardens, a children's playground and a mosque. The summit commands a panoramic view of Georgetown, the offshore islands lying north of Pulau Pinang and parts of the distant mainland, including Kedah Peak in Kedah. With temperatures hovering around twenty degrees centigrade, Penang Hill provides a cool retreat from the tropical warmth of the lowlands.

31 *(following page)* The funicular railway is presently the only mode of transport up Penang Hill. Opened in 1923, the Swiss-built railway is unique in the Far East for nowhere else except in Hong Kong can this type of railway be found. The railway operates in two sections and passengers have to change railcars at mid-point. The journey usually takes about 24 minutes. Apart from the funicular railway, there is also a large network of trails and footpaths leading to the West Peak, Strawberry Hill, Tiger Hill and other parts of the hill resort. At the foothill is Ayer Itam where the magnificent Kek Lok Si Temple is situated.

32 Fort Cornwallis marks the spot where the British led by Captain Francis Light landed to set up a settlement on Pulau Pinang in 1786. Constructed in 1810 to defend the harbour from enemy attacks, the original fort was a wooden structure. It was later replaced with the present stone structure built by convict labour. Today, only the outer walls of this fort remain. The area within the fort is now a park. Located here are a number of old cannons retrieved by the British from pirates who had captured them from the Johor Sultanate which was then a Dutch protectorate. The most famous is the Seri Rampai cannon which is believed to date back to 1613. According to old local beliefs, this ancient cannon had procreative powers and childless women could become fertile by placing flowers in its barrel and offering special prayers. Beside the fort is the Esplanade, a popular seafront for evening strollers to relax and taste some of the island's specialities.

33 To cater for the needs of export-oriented industries, the Malaysian Government has set up Free Trade Zones such as this in Bayan Lepas. Industries located in Free Trade Zones enjoy minimum customs formalities and duty-free imports of raw materials, component parts and machinery required directly in the manufacturing process. Since their inception in 1972, factories in Free Trade Zones have been contributing substantially to the country's export earnings. Today, Malaysia is the world's largest producer of electronic semi-conductors and the third largest producer of textile materials.

CHAPTER 2
Picturesque Malaysia

PERAK — The Tin State

No silver has ever been discovered, let alone mined, in Perak. But one can imagine the sheer joy of the first man who stumbled on alluvial tin in the Kinta Valley – to him and to the other miners who followed, tin was just as precious, as bright, as valuable as silver, that prince of metal. So we can perhaps forgive whoever dubbed the State as "Perak", meaning silver.

Concentrated within an area of 21,005 square kilometres, just north of Selangor and south of Kedah, Perak has the rare distinction of having the world's richest tin deposits inside its Kinta Valley. The state capital, Ipoh, sits in the midst of all these riches and is in fact, the town that tin built.

Another sort of 'riches' has also made the State somewhat famous. These are the limestones hills that ring Ipoh, many featuring huge, dark, echoing caves. Much like the famous Elephanta and Ajanta caves of India, these have acquired religious significance as well for Chinese and Indians. The bigger cave temples are good examples of how these caves can still be functional today – the Perak Tong and Sam Poh Tong, north and south of Ipoh respectively, are undoubtedly state landmarks. For a different sort of perspective, one that looks back 2,000 years to the Neolithic era, the Tambun aboriginal caves make one pause and ponder. Here are pre-historic rock paintings of deer, fish, lizards and Man etched in the crude, naive style of someone who has just discovered how to represent an object by drawing lines. Significantly, experts who have examined the cave drawings have remarked on the similarity with those discovered in South Africa and Australia, thus conferring on them the value of antiquity.

Switching back to the present, development in the State is being carried out apace. Most interesting of these projects is a recreational resort called Paradise Valley, now under way on a 43-hectare piece of reclaimed mining land. The resort is about 32 kilometres off the north-south trunk road leading to Ipoh.

North of Ipoh about 96 kilometres away is the old State capital of Taiping that offers diversion of a different kind. Its serenity is characterised by the Lake Gardens, showpiece of the town that once dominated the mines of the Larut district. Today, on each bank of the main lake a row of trees reach across with long, leafy bough to interlace and create a green bower. Here, time seems to linger while a steep ride in a jeep up 1,019 metres to Maxwell Hill brings a time-shift back to the old-world of leisurely tea in country cottages.

The pace picks up off the coast at Pulau Pangkor, an island resort with holiday accommodation from chalets to hotels. Adjacent to this main island is the smaller Pangkor Laut Resort, latest playground for those in search of sun and sea, a game of tennis or the pulsating rhythms of the disco. The more adventurous dive to a different beat at Emerald Bay where scuba diving and aquatic sports rule the day.

On shore at Lumut – the springboard to these resorts – lights go a-twinkle and the atmosphere turns carnival once a year as it hosts the annual Lumut Sea Festival. Fair ground activities, go-karting and sea sports, the crowds and the town's own beaches at Teluk Batik and Teluk Rubiah bustle with life.

Fortune has indeed smiled on this Tin State and its two million people continue to thrive.

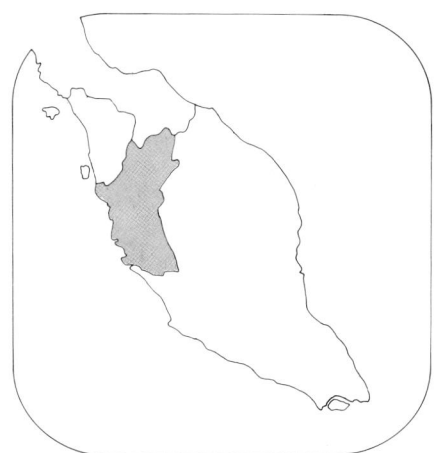

Tin dredging is presently the most modern method of extracting tin ore in Malaysia. Under this method of mining, a dredge floating on giant pontoons uses giant iron buckets to scoop tin-bearing earth from the bottom of a huge pit filled with water. The earth is then brought up to the dredge which also acts as an ore treatment plant. After the ore is extracted from the earth, the tailings (earth minus the tin ore) are then dumped at the back of the dredge to fill the area which has already been dredged.

35, 36 Perak, Malaysia's tin-state, contains the world's richest tin deposits in its Kinta Valley. Here, the gravel pump method is the main mode of extracting the precious ore. Powerful jets of water from monitors are used to loosen the earth in huge pits. The soil containing tin ore mixed with water is then pumped up wooden structures called *palong* or jig plants for treatments. However, due to the depletion of tin deposits in the state, many of these tin-mines have since been closed down. In view of the declining importance of the tin industry, which at one time contributed substantially to Perak's wealth, the state has embarked on a diversification programme to generate revenue from other sources. One such source that is becoming increasingly important is the tourism industry. New potential tourist spots, such as the 43-hectare Paradise Valley built on a piece of reclaimed mining land near Ipoh and the Pangkor Laut Resort, are identified and developed while existing ones, such as the Pangkor Island Resort, are upgraded to incorporate better amenities.

35   36

37 *(previous page)* Ipoh, the town that tin built, is located on the banks of the Kinta River in the Kinta Valley, the world's richest tin district. Popularly known as "Paloh" to the Chinese, Ipoh is Perak's capital and largest town. It is probably the best-planned town in the country as evidenced by its broad, well laid-out streets. The neo-classical colonial building on the left is the Ipoh Railway Station while the imposing building with numerous orange domes directly opposite it is the new state mosque. In the background is a magnificent backdrop of craggy limestone outcrops and the distant hills of the Keledang Range.

38 Taiping, the former capital of Perak, is one of the country's oldest tin-mining areas. Some of the earliest tin deposits which initiated the country's prosperous tin industry were first discovered in the Taiping district. Tin is still being mined here but its importance is slowly declining. Today, Taiping, which means "peaceful" in Chinese, is a relatively quiet down. Its Lake Gardens are among the country's largest and most attractive parks. Rising 1,019 metres behind the town is Bukit Larut or Maxwell Hill *(partly hidden in a shroud of thick clouds)*, the country's oldest hill resort.

39 Teluk Intan's prominent landmark is its leaning pagoda-shaped clock tower. It was built in 1890 as a memorial to Neol Denison, the then district superintendent of Lower Perak and Krian. During the Second World War, the authorities wanted to demolish the tower because it was feared that enemy bombers would use it as a landmark to bomb the town. The residents protested and the plan was later shelved.

40, 41 *(following two double-spread pages)* Teluk Intan, formerly known as Teluk Anson. The banks of this "sinking town" are gradually being eroded by the meandering Perak and Bidor Rivers. There was once a proposal to relocate this coastal town further inland but the plan was later shelved as it was too costly. The Government has instead allocated a large sum of money to straighten the meanders. Meanwhile, recent development is mainly concentrated further inland.

42 43

42 Kuala Kangsar, the royal town of Perak, lies on the banks of the Perak River. Two of Malaysia's first three rubber trees still stand in the District Office compound. Standing on a hillock called Bukit Chandan on the left banks of the river is Istana Iskandariah, the Sultan of Perak's official residence. Built in 1933, this imposing palace is greatly influenced by Indian-Islamic Saracenic designs incorporating architectural gems of Western Asia.

43 The Ubudiah Mosque, located opposite the Royal Mausoleum, was built by Sultan Idris Mursyidul Azam Shah, the 28th Ruler of Perak, to fulfil a vow. Completed in 1917, this stately mosque with its majestic golden dome is where all important Muslim celebrations in Kuala Kangsar are held.

44 45

44 Paddy fields in the Krian District, nicknamed the "Rice Bowl of Perak".

45 A newly-constructed irrigation canal supplying water to paddy fields in the Krian district. The narrow earth bunds on both sides of the canal are often used as "roads" by the farmers.

46 *(following page)* Pangkor town and its busy pier on a Sunday.

47 Located about six kilometres south of Ipoh is a huge limestone outcrop housing a few cave temples. The largest and most popular is the Sam Poh Tong Temple located in a hollowed-out centre with perpendicular cliffs about 60 metres high. At the end of the temple, which houses over 30 statues of the Lord Buddha, is a short narrow tunnel leading to a huge opening surrounded by limestone cliffs. Here, there is a pond full of turtles. In the foreground *(with concrete roof)* are stalls selling pomeloes, one of Ipoh's specialities.

48 Kellie's Castle is an old abandoned, half-completed mansion nestling in dense undergrowth beside the road from Batu Gajah to the Ipoh-Kuala Lumpur highway. Named after its owner, William Kellie Smith, Kellie's Castle was built in 1915 but it was never completed. The mansion has trap doors and hidden stairs leading down to darkened basements and wine cellars.

49 *(previous page)* Pangkor Island, lying off the Perak coast, is about twelve kilometres long and four kilometres wide. Pangkor town, the biggest of the island's three fishing towns, is located to the right of the jungle clearing. The other two towns, Sungei Pinang Kecil and Sungei Pinang Besar, are situated further up the coast. Historically, Pangkor Island was the venue for the signing of the Pangkor Treaty in 1874 on board a British warship anchored off the island which paved the way for the appointment of a British Resident in Perak.
Today, the island is being developed into a major beach resort. An airstrip for light aircraft is also under construction. The small island lying off Pangkor Island is Pangkor Laut Island.

50 Emerald Bay, an unnaturally natural submarine cove, situated on Pangkor Laut Island. Before the Pangkor Laut Resort was developed, this isolated bay was only accessible by boats from Pasir Bogak. Now, it is just a ten-minute trek from the resort.

51 *(following page)* Pangkor Laut, a small jungle-clad island opposite Pangkor Island's Pasir Bogak Beach. Located at Royal Bay is Pangkor Laut Resort, one of Malaysia's latest seaside resorts. This newly-opened resort, run club-style, has a 75-room hotel, tennis courts beside the sea and a host of other modern amenities.

CHAPTER 2
Picturesque Malaysia

SELANGOR DARUL EHSAN
— The Opportunity Land

Of the 14 points on the star featured in the country's flag (each point representing one of the 13 states and the 14th point representing the Federal Government), probably none glows more brightly than that symbolizing Selangor. For within a compact 24,500 square kilometres, Selangor has been blessed with its share of natural and man-made spectacles worthy of a leading state.

Like many of the west coast states of Peninsular Malaysia, Selangor sits snugly sheltered by the hazy blue mountains of the Main Range, that swathe of highlands ridging down the centre of the peninsula. The Main Range protects the state's 1.6 million people from the full, devastating fury of those year-end, flood-creating storms, the North East Monsoon.

Most famous of the state's natural attractions is Batu Caves. While not as massive as the White Cliffs of Dover, the Batu Caves' claim to fame is still well-substantiated – especially the white roofed Cathedral Cave (because someone thought it resembled St. Peter's Cathedral) wherein the Hindu deity, Lord Subramaniam, is serene in his shrine. It is to pay homage to him that every year during Thaipusam thousands of Hindus ascend the forbiddingly steep flight of 272 steps leading to this shrine. It is a sight to wonder at as wave upon wave of men, women and children slowly float up, many with their bodies pierced with spikes and skewers as part of fulfilling a vow in return for favours asked and received. At times like this, the air is thick with heavy incense and religious fervour burns in every eye.

A second impressive mass of limestone outcrops is located some eight kilometres from Batu Caves in the 1,214-hectare Templer Park. Named after Tan Sri Gerald Templer, the last British Commissioner in the Federation of Malaya, the park counts among its many attractions the 305-metre high Bukit Takun (Takun Hill) and Anak Takun (Takun Child). The former is believed to date back 400 million years to the Silurian Age and today is home to 204 species of flowering and non-flowering plants, of which 17 are unique to this part of the world. The smaller Takun has a network of caves and fossils that have remained largely intact, a record of its history.

Apart from these glimpses of the past, the Park is also alive with a vast number of birds, animals and butterflies sometimes encountered on its jungle paths. In particular, the beautiful Raja Brooke Birdwing butterfly can be spotted basking beside fresh, clear water streams.

Of the many man-made marvels, one is the open-cast tin mine at Sungei Besi – still working and reputed as one of the world's largest. Another wondrous work of man is at Shah Alam, the state capital. Here, a state mosque dominates the skyline with its arresting electric blue dome overlaid with shiny, steel latticework. And, like the open cast mine, it goes down in recent history as being even larger than the dome of the world renowned St. Paul's Cathedral in London.

In the opposite direction from Shah Alam, towards the hills and just 18 kilometres from Kuala Lumpur is Mimaland, or 'Miniature Malaysia Land'. Carved from the jungle and on the road to the country's only casino-in-the-sky at Genting Highlands, Mimaland is a coolly pleasant day or weekend spot. Diversions like boating and a lazy swim in the sprawling pool or venturing among pre-historic animal sculptures are but a few available. But if preference runs to viewing live animals and marine life, then the National Zoo and Aquarium at Ulu Kelang are the solution.

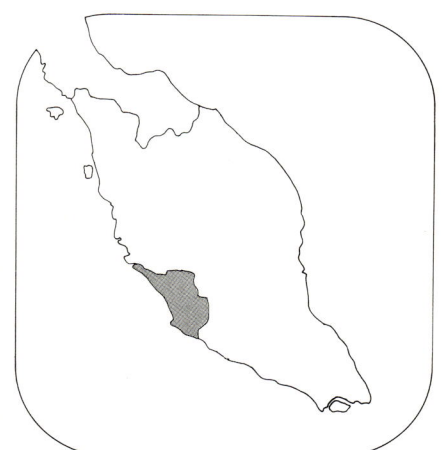

Kota Darul Ehsan or "The Bastion of Selangor", a monumental archway across the Kuala Lumpur – Kelang Federal Highway that acts as a border separating the state of Selangor Darul Ehsan from the Federal Territory of Kuala Lumpur. This four million ringgit grand marble arch has four century-old cannons retrieved from a fort in Kuala Selangor.

(continued from previous page)

A thriving, growing state just beginning to hit its stride, Selangor also has its share of historic towns. The royal town of Kelang was the scene of many a war in the past over tin mines; Port Kelang as Port Swettenham dates back to the time of the British Residents (and perhaps before); Morib, an old-time beach resort still popular today; and Kuala Selangor with its fort, cannons and lighthouse of a bygone era.

All things considered, it is clear the state is rightly regarded as the leading star in the country.

53 The Kuala Lumpur International Airport at Subang is Malaysia's biggest and most sophisticated airport. Completed in 1965, the airport's original terminal was given a major facelift and became fully functional again in 1983. An additional terminal handling mainly chartered and Haj pilgrimage flights was recently built about 1.6 kilometres from the original terminal. To meet the demand of increasing traffic at this busy airport, a second runway has been planned by the authorities.

54 Top view of the Malaysian Airline System (MAS) cargo centre, the pride of MASKARGO. Fully automated and equipped with the latest computer system, this ultra-modern complex can handle 300,000 tons of cargo annually and is geared to meet the significant growth expected in cargo traffic up to the 1990s.

55 B747 Rolls Royce engine under inspection in the MAS power plant workshop. MAS engineering services are now available at a new multi-million ringgit engineering complex which stands proud at the Kuala Lumpur International Airport at Subang. This column free hangar-cum-workshop has the capacity to accommodate a B747, a DC-10 and two B737s at any one time.

56 *(following page)* About 30 years ago, a settlement for squatters made up of a series of ramshackled huts was started about six kilometres away from Kuala Lumpur. Within the next three decades, factories germinated, government quarters and high-rise buildings sprouted, houses built and population increased by the thousands, transforming this area into the country's biggest satellite town. This is Petaling Jaya, whose residents now have the country's highest per capita income and where signs of affluence are marked by impressive bungalows, shopping complexes and growing industrialization.

57 Steel bars being produced at a factory in the Bukit Raja Industrial Area in the Kelang Valley. The steel and iron industry began in Malaysia about the same time as the tin mining industry, mainly to produce cast iron parts to serve the tin mines. Today, the industry covering manufacturing activities such as bar mill and secondary wire products, iron and steel castings and flat and secondary sheet products is part of the country's heavy industries programme.

58 The Malaysian car, Proton Saga, is manufactured at the Perusahaan Otomobil Nasional factory (*left*) situated in the Heavy Industries Corporation of Malaysia (Hicom) Industrial Estate in Shah Alam. Across the road in the foreground is the Edaran Otomobil Nasional (EON) building. Cars from the factory are driven across the flyover (*centre*) to the EON building to be fitted with accessories followed by final checking before they are sent to showrooms. The car project, a joint venture between Hicom, Mitsubishi Corporation and Mitsubishi Motors Corporation of Japan, is part of Malaysia's industrialization programme and the brainchild of the Malaysian Prime Minister, Datuk Seri Dr Mahathir Mohamad.

59 *(page 90, 91)* Shah Alam, formerly known as Sungei Renggam, was commissioned Selangor's new capital on December 7, 1978 after its former capital, Kuala Lumpur, was turned into a Federal Territory in 1974. Within a short span of time, it has developed into an important commercial and industrial town as well as a residential and educational centre in the Kelang Valley. In the foreground on the left is part of the Batu Tiga Racing Circuit where motor racing at national and international levels is held. The building with Minangkabau-style roofs beside the racing circuit on the right is Kelab Sultan Alam Shah. Situated on a hillock across the mainroad behind the club is the Istana Kayangan, the official residence of the Sultan of Selangor. The building with a huge electric blue dome under construction on the extreme right is the Masjid Sultan Salahuddin, one of the world's largest mosques. Next to the mosque is the multi-million dollar Shah Alam lake, which is divided into the Central, Western and Eastern sections.

60 *(previous page)* The royal town of Kelang is one of Malaysia's oldest towns. Artefacts discovered here revealed that man first occupied Kelang about 2,000 years ago and the first written documents on this historical town date back to the Majapahit rule about 600 years ago. Relics of the town's rich historic past include the Raja Mahdi fort and the Warehouse of Raja Abdullah, the oldest building in Kelang which was used as an arsenal during the civil wars of the 1860s. The magnificent building overlooking a sprawling field on the left is Istana Alam Shah, the Sultan of Selangor's palace.

61 Port Kelang, located about 40 kilometres from Kuala Lumpur, is the country's premier port serving the highly industrialized Kelang Valley and its hinterland such as the southern part of Perak in the north and Gemas in the south. Its inland port, now known as the South Port, is located at the estuary of the Kelang River. It handles all export and import cargoes such as wheat grain and petroleum products.

62 *(page 95)* The North Port is located 6.4 kilometres from the South Port. There are 18 berths with a total quay length of 3,858 metres. Located here are the container terminal, dry bulk terminal, liquid bulk terminal and the conventional traffic area. This deep water port (13.4 metres deep) can accommodate third generation container vessels to berth even at low tide. The North Kelang by-pass connects the port to the city.

63 *(page 96, 97)* A ship navigating the narrow channel off Port Kelang and heading towards the Straits of Malacca, one of the four maritime gateways to the world's oceans (the others are the Panama Canal, Suez Canal and Gibraltar Straits). Also known as the Suez of South-East Asia, the 976-kilometre long Straits of Malacca is the world's longest strait.

64 *(page 98, 99)* Literally translated, Pulau Ketam means crab island. Located five kilometres off the coast of Selangor, this island is the home of about 20,000 people whose wooden houses are built on stilts. Fishing is the main occupation here.

65 Kajang, located about 22 kilometres south of Kuala Lumpur, is famous for its *satay* – delicious morsels of beef, lamb or chicken barbequed Malaysian-style served with spicy chilli sauce mixed with peanuts.

66 *(following page)* Kuala Selangor is 64 kilometres north-west of Kuala Lumpur This grand old riverine town built on the south banks of the Selangor river exudes an aura of exigent lore and legends. The relics of its rich historic past include the Kota Malawati (Fort Altingsburg), believed to be built during the reign of the second Sultan of Selangor (1778-1826), Batu Hampar (execution block) and the Seven Wells. The gleaming white lighthouse is the most prominent landmark which can be seen for kilometres around.

67 *(page 104, 105)* These lush green paddy fields in Sekinchan typify the many paddy fields in Malaysia. Paddy planters here live in a close-knit community. The straight coastal road connects Sekinchan to most of the towns on the west coast of the country.

68 69

68, 69 Rubber plantations such as this can be spotted in most parts of the country, especially along the west coast of the peninsula. Young rubber trees like these in the picture mature to neck-stretching heights in five years. The rubber industry has undergone numerous changes since the first rubber seedlings were brought into the country by H.N. Ridley. Recently, the country's Rubber Research Institute (RRI) succeeded in producing "test-tube" rubber trees through cell-culture techniques. Today, Malaysia is the world's largest producer of natural rubber, contributing to about 36.5 per cent of the total world supply of this useful commodity. Latex is extracted from the rubber trees using a metal tapping knife. Most of the rubber tappers in the country are women.

70 *(previous page)* This gigantic limestone outcrop is a prominent landmark near the Selangor-Kuala Lumpur border. Located within this majestic outcrop is a fine network of caverns known as the Batu Caves. The main cavern, the Cathedral Cave, with its huge stalactite that hangs about six metres down, houses a shrine of the Hindu deity, Lord Subramaniam. Twenty other caverns of relatively easy access can also be found here. Midget Hindu deities and plaster figures are located in one of the small caves nearby the illuminated Dark Caves. The prominent white scar on the face of the outcrop is caused by quarrying which has since stopped. A gravel pump tin mine, one of the methods for extracting tin ore, is still in operation nearby.

71 The No. 2 Open Cast Hong Fatt Pit at Sungei Besi Mines Malaysia Berhad. Started in 1909 after rich tin deposits were discovered in the area, the mine is now reputed to be one of the world's largest dry tin mines both in terms of area and output via a dry-dredging system. The pit is more than 160 metres deep and covers an area of about eight square kilometres. Under the present system of mining, tin-bearing earth is excavated from the bottom of the pit using a hydraulic shovel. The tin-bearing earth is then transported by trucks to a stockpile. It is later transferred by bucket wheel excavators onto a conveyor belt system to be sent to a treatment plant where the ore is extracted.

71 72
73

72, 73 Mimaland or "Miniature Malaysia Land" is a 121-hectare tourist complex lying about 18 kilometres from Kuala Lumpur. Its recreational facilities include a sprawling natural swimming pool, well-kept jungle paths and a huge lake for boating and fishing. Accommodation is available in motel rooms and *bagan* or chalets built on stilts at the edge of the lake.

74, 75 Giraffes and peacocks at the National Zoo in Ulu Kelang. Situated on 26 hectares of shady forest land with a central lake, the zoo is nicknamed "zoo in the jungle" because of its lush green rainforest backdrop where birdcalls can be heard. Besides giraffes and peacocks, the zoo has over 200 species of Malaysian animals, birds and reptiles as well as a representative collection of species from all over the world. Among them are the orang utan, gir lion and other rare mammals like the *selembu*, a cross breed between the domestic cow and *seladang* (buffaloes).

74   75

76 This Kelang Gate limestone ridge rising to about 250 metres above sea level forms one of the main water catchment areas supplying water to many parts of the Kelang Valley. There are numerous trails beside the dam leading to the ridge where there is a waterfall. At the foothill on the left is Taman Melawati, one of the city's many housing estates.

CHAPTER 2
Picturesque Malaysia

NEGERI SEMBILAN — The Minangkabau State

What sets this state apart from the others is its distinctive Minangkabau heritage which is externalized in the unique architecture of the traditional homes. Negeri Sembilan – which means "nine states" – extends over an area of 6,600 square kilometres with inhabitants numbering 700,000. Of these, the majority of the Malays are of Minang descent, their forefathers being pioneers from Minangkabau in West Sumatra who crossed the Straits to settle here around 1600 A.D. The customs, laws and oral tradition are of a different cast, one of the main features being matriarchy in which women inherit property and land over the men.

The other distinctive feature of the Minangkabau legacy is the smoothly swooping, perfectly balanced points on the roofs of the traditional houses, resembling the buffalo's horns after which they are fashioned. An outstanding example of Minangkabau style is in the Handicraft Complex of Taman Seni Budaya in Seremban. Also situated here are the State Museum and an original Minangkabau house built without the reinforcement of a single iron or metal brace. In the royal town of Sri Menanti is the Istana Sri Menanti, a beautifully carved wooden palace built in 1902.

Still in search of history, the visitor can stop off near Pengkalan Kempas to ponder on some large, mysterious megaliths. There they stand, about two metres high, inside a roofed pavilion standing on a two-hectare compound. Believed to be pre-Hindu, these megaliths are still baffling the experts.

Of more recent history is the Lukut Fort built in the 1820s by Raja Jumaat. It is sited on Bukit Gajah Mati, slightly off the trunk road that links Seremban with its famous beach resort, Port Dickson.

In the opposite direction, at Kuala Pilah, there is a large memorial to Martin Lister, who was the state's first British Resident. He is credited with helping to unify the state under its various rulers.

Seremban, the state capital, began as a tin mining town about 100 years ago. Its lake garden is the central feature, providing a welcome breath of green. Also located here is the State Mosque with its nine pillars representing the nine ancient sultanates of Sungai Hujung, (now part of Kelang), Jelebu, Rembau (which includes Tampin), Naning (forming part of Melaka today), Segamat and Pasir Besar (both in Johor), Jelai, Ina and Hulu Pahang (now incorporated into Pahang).

Port Dickson, the favourite playground of Kuala Lumpur residents, is just 25 minutes' drive away from Seremban. The attraction is its 18-kilometre sandy beaches, ending on a headland with a lighthouse dating back to the 16th century. The resort is fast developing into a mini-version of Waikiki beach with condominiums, hotels and time-share holiday resorts springing up at a mind-boggling rate. Meanwhile, with land reclamation projects under way, it will be only a matter of time before a Malaysian-style Disneyland takes shape.

These original nine states with the Minangkabau heritage have given Malaysia not just its most sought-after resort but also helped enrich the cultural polyglot that exists in the country.

The town of Port Dickson.

78 *(previous page)* Seremban, the capital of Negeri Sembilan, is the administrative, financial and commercial centre of the state. Despite rapid development especially over the last decade, this progressive town still retains "lungs" of greenery such as its sprawling Lake Gardens located in a valley. Also situated here are the state museum and a model house built without a single nail, typifying the traditional Minangkabau architecture.

79 This stretch of lovely sandy beaches from the 9th-kilometre Port Dickson road to the headland of Cape Rachardo is very popular to weekend trippers from Kuala Lumpur. Located here is Si-Rusa Inn and the Ming Court Beach Hotel besides the numerous private holiday chalets and condominiums.

80 Low tide on a secluded beach at Port Dickson. Hermit crabs which inhabit the seaside shores surface from their homes to forage for food. The little balls of sand they create form interesting intricate patterns on the shore.

81 *(following page)* A breath-taking view of Port Dickson's white sandy beaches from 1,300 metres above sea level. In the foreground is Tanjung Tuan while Port Dickson's harbour and town are situated on the promontory further up the coast. A number of land reclamation projects are now underway along the coast, especially near the town. Among the proposed projects are a Malaysian-style Disneyland, time-sharing beach hotels and condominiums. Located further inland here are the Shell and Esso oil refineries.

82 *(page 124, 125)* An oil refinery in Port Dickson. Although a net exporter of petroleum, Malaysia still imports crude oil to be refined for local consumption. This is because the country's crude oil which is of high quality earns handsome foreign exchange in the world market.

CHAPTER 2
Picturesque Malaysia

MELAKA — Birthplace of the Nation

When Parameswara, the Sumatran prince attributed with the founding of Malacca, settled on his chosen spot, he could hardly have suspected the glory-years that were to follow. This historic repository of Peninsular Malaysia covering just 1,650 square kilometres of the country was a great port in the competitive maritime era. So famous, indeed, that it was fought over by the Portuguese, Dutch and the British as each in succession jealously sought to control its entrepot trade. Fittingly, it was also the site on which the country's first Prime Minister Tunku Abdul Rahman together with thousands of people gathered to proclaim independence from the British on February 20, 1956.

Today, the past is very much a part of the present in Melaka town, relics of famous ruins adjoining more recent structures. In the centre of the older part of the town, the Dutch Stadthuys or Town Hall erected as early as the 1640s together with Christ Church built in 1753 are fine examples of Dutch architecture. The Portuguese legacy is less intact – the famed formidable fortress of A Famosa which repelled many attacks for 130 years is reduced to the Porta De Santiago while St. Paul's Church on the summit of St. Paul's Hill is but bare walls and ruins. It was once here that St. Francis Xavier preached a sermon and where his body was briefly interred before being taken to its final resting place in Goa, India.

Pre-dating these colonial structures are Bukit China and the Perigi Raja or Sultan's Well. Bukit China marks the spot where Chinese officials first stepped on Malacca when they accompanied their princess given as a bride to Sultan Mansur Shah. Today the hill is the largest Chinese cemetery outside China with graves that date back to the Ming Dynasty. The Sultan's Well nearby is reputed never to run dry and visitors who drink its waters will surely make a return visit.

Since historic Melaka has been under so many different cultural influence, it is little wonder that its antiquities, people and customs are quite unique. Inter-marriage between the early Portuguese and the local residents has produced Portuguese Eurasians who perpetuate the customs and religious festivals of their forefathers. The seat of this sub-group of Malaysians is at the Portuguese Settlement set up by the British in 1931. Another sub-culture are the Babas and Nyonyas whose roots trace back to the middle of the fifteenth century when the Chinese princess, Hang Li-Po arrived as bride to Sultan Mansur Shah. Members of her entourage inter-married with the Malays and thus the Straits-born or *peranakan* Chinese evolved. These Babas-Nyonyas, dying out today, reflect the Sino-Malay influences in their customs, food and rites. A private museum known as the Baba Nyonya Heritage is open along Jalan Tun Tan Cheng Lock where intricately carved, mother-of-pearl furniture and artefacts are on view.

Antique-hunting along Jalan Hang Jebat, visits to the oldest Chinese temple, the Cheng Hoon Teng, the Tranquerah Mosque, the Padang Pahlawan (Warrior's Field) where Independence was proclaimed, the Melaka Museum, and the beaches at Tanjung Bidara, Klebang Besar and Tanjung Kling constitute other memorable places of interest.

Perhaps no other state in Malaysia so encapsulates the nation's historic pulse as Melaka, still vibrant, still serene after its turbulent past.

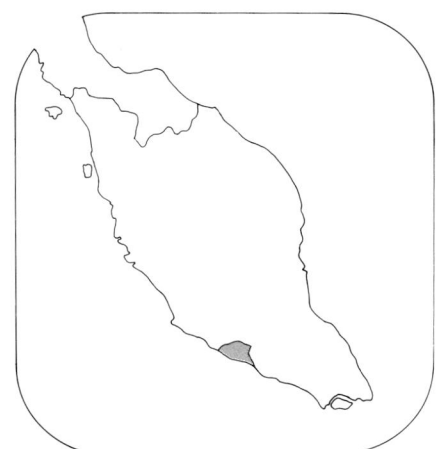

The Porta De Santiago or the Gateway of St James at the foot of St Paul's Hill in Bandar Hilir. This formidable stone bastion is the only vestige of the A Famosa erected by the Portuguese during their occupation of Melaka (1511 – 1641). It was badly damaged during the Dutch attack prior to their capture of the land in 1641. It was further destroyed by the British when they succeeded the Dutch in 1824. However, the timely arrival of Sir Stamford Raffles, the founder of Singapore, prevented it from being totally destroyed.

84 Part of the ruins of St Paul's Church on top of St Paul's Hill. Built in 1521, the original building was a leading Catholic chapel before it was renamed St Paul's Church when the Dutch captured Melaka from the Portuguese in 1641. The Dutch used it until 1753 when they moved to a new church and it was relegated to a burial ground for their notables. St Francis Xavier, the missionary who brought Catholicism to this part of the world in the mid-sixteenth century, was temporarily buried here before his body was sent to Goa, India. There is an open grave covered with wire mesh to mark the spot where the saint was buried. There are also several huge tombstones from the sixteenth century with Latin, Portuguese and Dutch inscriptions.

85 This clock-tower is part of the Red Square (the Stadthuys) and the passing minutes registered on its clocks each day prompt reminders of the Stadthuys' 300-odd-year existence.

86 A pleasant and leisurely way to sightsee Melaka is by taking a sedate ride in a trishaw. In the background is part of the Stadthuys, a Dutch relic.

87 This fountain was built by the local residents to commemorate Queen Victoria's Diamond Jubilee (1837-1897) during the British occupation of Melaka. In the background is the Melaka main post office located within the Red Square. The Red Square, flanked by the Melaka River on one side and part of St Paul's Hill on the other, comprises the post office, the Stadthuys, the Christ Church and the clock-tower. All these structures, painted red since the Dutch occupation days, form a distinct landmark in the heart of the town.

88 St Peter's Church, one of the Portuguese relics in Melaka. It was built in 1710 after the Dutch restored Catholicism to the Portuguese. Before the church was built, Dutch reformers forbade the Portuguese from practising their Catholic faith and Catholics were forced to hold religious services in the forests. The facade of the church is an interesting combination of Oriental and Occidental architecture. The chapel has some noteworthy stained glass decorations and old tombstones.

89 The Melaka Museum is housed in the Stadthuys, one of the Dutch relics. The wide range of exhibits on display in the museum trace Melaka's history from the ancient Malay kingdom through Portuguese, Dutch, British occupation to its present position as a Malaysian state.

87 88 89

90 *(following page)* Bandar Hilir – the historical section of Melaka town where many relics of the Dutch and Portuguese era such as the Stadthuys and the ruins of A Famosa are located. In the centre is St Paul's Hill where the ruins of the famous St Paul's Church are located. Under construction at the foot of the hill is the Melaka Sultanate Palace Complex. The complex will comprise a replica of a fifteenth century palace modelled after Sultan Mansur Shah's residence about 500 years ago, as described in the Malay annals, and also a restaurant constructed in the style of a kampung house.

91, 93, 94, 95 Every year from June 29 to July 1, the Portuguese Settlement in Melaka is turned into a carnival ground. Joined by their relatives and friends from all over Malaysia and abroad, the Portuguese Eurasians here (the descendants of Portuguese who married local residents during the former's 130-year rule of Melaka) celebrate Festa San Pedro or Festival of St Peter in honour of the patron saint of fisher folk.

This three-day festival is a grand celebration of dances, songs and feasting. It is also an occasion for the annual boat-decorating contest where boats are gaily decorated with colourful flags, buntings and biblical verses.

92 Reverend James Chan, the Bishop of Melaka and Johor blessing a fleet of gaily decorated fishing boats after a High Mass, a tradition that dates back five centuries to the era of Portuguese discoveries. The participants of this annual boat-decorating contest take great pains to ensure that their humble fishing boats appear like huge galleons.

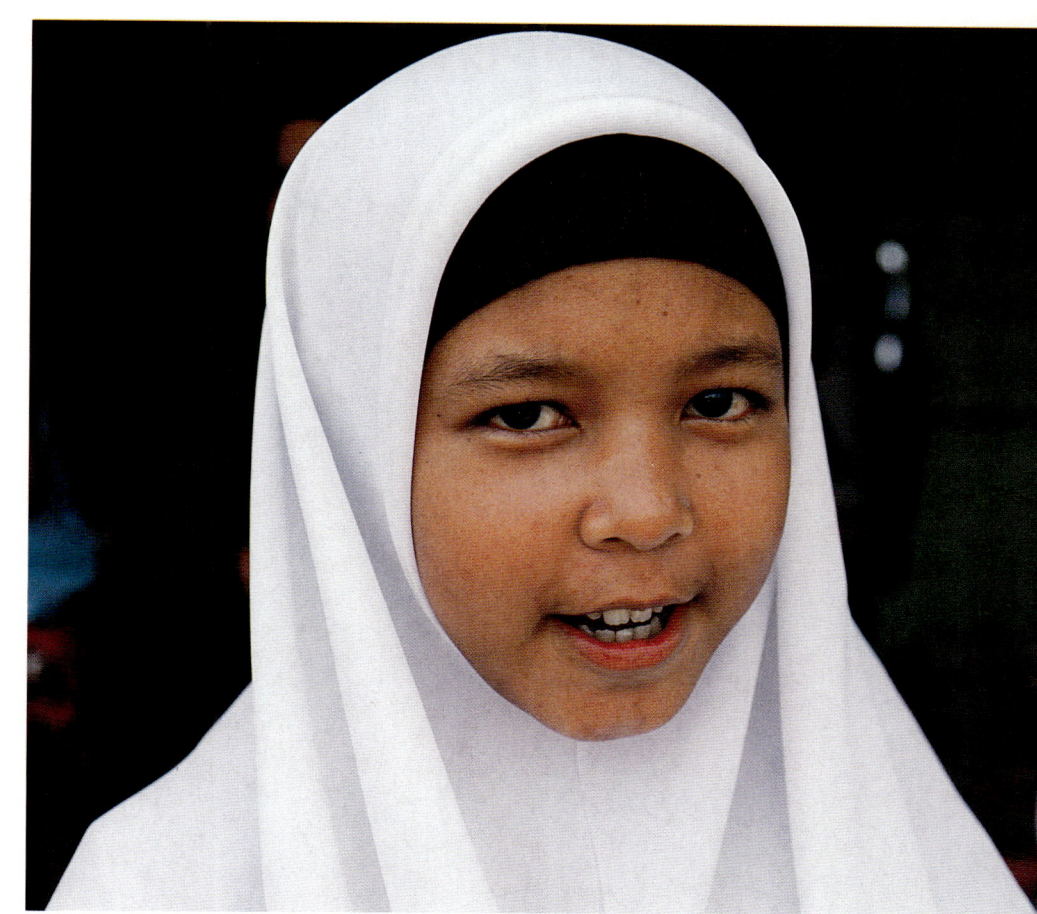

96 The Church of St Francis is a prominent landmark near the Melaka River. Under the Portuguese, missionaries like the famous St Francis Xavier strove to spread Christianity in Melaka. As a result, some of the local residents were converted.

97 For many Muslim girls like this, the proper dress code in accordance with Islamic practices is taught from a very young age. The girl's wimple-like head-dress is known as a *tudung*.

98 Kampung Keling Mosque is a Sumatran-style mosque located in the older section of Melaka town. Melaka played an important role in the propagation of Islam in the Malay Peninsula and South-East Asia. Islam became Melaka's official religion during the reign of Sultan Muzaffar Shah (1445-1459).

100

99 *(previous page)* A North-South view of Melaka town with large areas of land reclaimed from the sea off its seafront on the right. Part of this reclaimed land is the site of the Melaka Jaya project next to Padang Pahlawan (Warrior's Field). The skyline of the town, especially its main commercial centre, has changed considerably over the last few years. A number of high-rise buildings such as the newly-opened Ramada Renaissance Hotel have sprung up, providing a stark contrast to the surrounding old shophouses. Bukit China, reputedly the largest Chinese burial ground outside mainland China, is situated north of Ramada Hotel. In the foreground is the Kubu Stadium, the state's main stadium. Off the coast is Pulau Besar where a multi-million ringgit holiday resort is being built.

100 A traditional wedding ceremony of the Straits-born Chinese of Sino-Malay descent is a colourful and elaborate affair. This Baba-Nyonya (a male Straits-born is called a Baba while his female counterpart is known as a Nyonya) wedding ceremony with all its traditions and detailed procedures can last twelve full days. Like many aspects of their way of life, the Baba-Nyonya matrimonial practices are in many ways influenced by Malay culture. With the gradual influence of Western culture, this sub-culture is dying out.

101 Although Islam is Malaysia's official religion, the country's Constitution guarantees religious freedom for all. Here, two Buddhist monks are meditating inside the 340-year-old Cheng Hoon Teng Temple in Melaka, the country's oldest Chinese temple.

101

102 Jalan Hang Jebat (formerly Jongker Street) where a wide range of antiques can be bought. The Malaysian flags in front of the shops were hoisted during the twenty-eighth National Day celebrations which were held outside Kuala Lumpur for the first time.

103 Many of the shops along Jonker Street sell antiques: Indian oil-lamps, brass-urns, Chinese nuptial beds and opium benches, mother-of-pearl furniture and *chaise longue*, malay *keris*, nyonya ornaments, grandfather clocks, altar tables and incense burners. These antiques shed some light on Malaysia's rich historic past. And nestling in between these collectors' items are other antiquity of Portuguese, Dutch and even Victorian origins.

102   103

104 *(previous page)* Malaysia's Supreme Head of State, His Majesty the Yang di-Pertuan Agong (in light blue bush jacket), taking the salute as members of the Malaysian army march past the VIP stand during National Day celebrations at Padang Pahlawan in Melaka on August 31, 1985. Standing alongside the Agong (King) are the Prime Minister, members of his Cabinet, the Melaka Chief Minister and state officials.

105 A group of schoolchildren performing the Belantari, a dance using Indian clubs, during the twenty-eighth National Day celebrations at Padang Pahlawan (Warriors' Field). In the background is the Independence Memorial Hall, formerly the Melaka Club building. The Memorial Hall is a salute to the nation's leaders who struggled and secured Malaya's independence from the British. Foremost amongst them is Tunku Abdul Rahman, the leader of the Independence Delegation to London who later became the country's first Prime Minister. On display in the Hall are artefacts, photographs, documents and other memorabilia associated with the struggle for independence, including the historic car used by the Tunku when he arrived at Padang Pahlawan to proclaim independence on February 20, 1956.

106 Another group of schoolchildren in colourful track suits putting up a callisthenics display, one of the highlights of the 1985 National Day Celebrations.

105 106

107 108
109

107 Tranquil Malay fishing villages such as this in Klebang Besar adorn the coasts of Melaka. To supplement their incomes, some of the fishermen plant paddy and coconut trees. Rice is the staple food of the villagers while coconuts are used for cooking curry and numerous other Malay dishes.

108 A typical Malay house in Melaka with a grand tiled staircase. The house is usually built on stilts and has many windows. The space under the house is often used as a store and for drying clothes especially during rainy season and sometimes for afternoon naps too. The open windows ensure that the house is well ventilated and cool, even on hot days.

109 A Melakan fisherman sorting out his catch.

110 Air Keroh is an industrial and tourist centre located about 13 kilometres from Melaka town. In the foreground is the Air Keroh Country Club with its golf course. Across the lake is the Melaka Village Resort. Also located here is the 16-hectare Melaka Zoo which will soon be extended to cover 30 hectares to be developed along the open safari concept. The "Malaysia in Miniature" Cultural Village with houses typifying the country's diverse cultures is also in this vicinity.

111 Pulau Besar resembles a giant sting-ray at 1,300 metres above sea-level. Lying about 17 kilometres off the coast of Melaka, this relatively unexplored island is a revered place with numerous *makam* or shrines whose origins have yet to be established. The main shrine is dedicated to Almarhum Sultan Arifin Sikh Ismail, a Muslim missionary who is believed to have come from the Middle East about 700 years ago. During weekends, large crowds gather to pray at these shrines. This serene island is presently being developed into a sprawling holiday resort.

112 Tucked away in all its natural beauty on the northeast of Melaka town is the Durian Tunggal dam and catchment area. In the vicinity is the 62-hectare Durian Tunggal Recreation Park, a popular picnic spot for local residents to indulge in boating, fishing and camping.

CHAPTER 2
Picturesque Malaysia

JOHOR — Land's End of Mainland Asia

The large land mass of continental Asia, after cutting across so many time zones and climatic variations, reaches its most southerly point in the tapered end of Johor. This southernmost state of Peninsular Malaysia covering 19,000 square kilometres is an area of mixed agriculture. Short, spiky clumps of pineapples grown mostly for canning and destined for foreign markets together with oil palm and rubber trees are common sights flanking the south trunk road that culminates in the 1,000 metre long Causeway into Singapore.

As a tourist stop, Johor's offerings are anything but sparing. A few kilometres north of the state capital of Johor Baharu is a 311-hectare drive-in animal park. This last "frontier" for 100 wild animals, ranging from ponzi to Bengal tigers, giraffes to the rare white rhinoceroses, is the only one in South-East Asia. Deliberately, the Johor Safari World is set in rugged terrain not unlike the natural habitat of the animals. Within the park, too, is a Fiesta Village where performing parrots and gorillas regularly steal the show. A 350-metre long roller coaster track and a cinema with a 180-degree screen are the other attractions in the village.

A second project is under way along the border with Pahang where a last refuge for threatened species of flora and fauna in Peninsular Malaysia will eventually take hold. The Endau-Rompin National Park, as it will be called, will protect the 84,000 hectares of lowland tropical rainforest from development. Here, the last few Sumatran rhinoceroses can roam in unharassed peace while the forests themselves, which have remained untouched for at least 130 million years, will continue intact for posterity.

Moving out of the wild and into the towns, the state capital, Johor Baharu is a pleasant stopover. Built in 1855 by the then reigning Sultan, it is far from being a "frontier" town; instead, it is awash in places old and new, some rambling and charming, others of the super-high rise variety with sparkling towers. A stroller's promenade often draws crowds out for a breath of air while the Istana Besar or Principal Palace of the Johor royal family perched on a hill behind the promenade is a joy to explore. The landscaped garden, the Victorian-style architecture, the museum within housing priceless items, the grand throne room and banquet hall never fail to draw admiring gasps.

Johor Baharu or New Johor actually came about because the traditional seat of the royal family at Johor Lama (Old Johor) was destroyed in the sixteenth century. The old village is on the Johor River, about 30 kilometres from the capital, and its fort has since been restored.

For those in search of a tan, the Desaru resort on the southeast coast and about an hour's drive away, is the best answer. It is newly developed and has practically something for everyone, a 18-hole course for avid golfers; great opportunities for swimming, snorkelling, canoeing or fishing; docile ponies for rides on the beach or on jungle paths; even camping facilities if the rugged life is preferred.

Northwards from Desaru is Mersing where just 16 kilometres off-shore is the tiny but serene Pulau Rawa, a coral island with first-class diving, fishing and scenes for underwater photography, given its rich and varied coral reef marine life.

Kota Tinggi, on the other hand, is freshwater country with its astounding waterfalls thundering from 37 metres up. Kukup, the fishing village is famous by virtue of its affordably-priced fresh seafood, while Ayer Hitam has carved its name in ceramics being the place where the Aw potters work their magic on clay.

A journey to Johor may, at one level, mean the end of the road from mainland Asia but with its endless variety it seems but the beginning of a world of enjoyment.

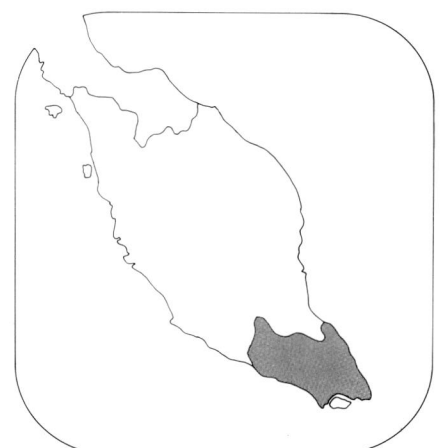

This Saracenic-style building on Bukit Timbalan, houses the offices of both the State and Federal Governments. Johor Baharu has been the state's administrative centre since 1855 when the late Sultan Abu Bakar moved the capital from Johor Lama (Old Johor), a small village on the Johor River, about 30 kilometres from the present capital.

114 Johor Baharu (New Johor), the state capital of Johor, was built in 1855 by the late Sultan Abu Bakar after the traditional seat of the royal family at Johor Lama (Old Johor) was destroyed in the sixteenth century. This progressive town is the southern gateway to Peninsular Malaysia and is connected to Singapore *(in the background)* by road and rail via a 1,000-metre long causeway.

115 The fishing port of Mersing, situated about 136 kilometres northeast of Johor Baharu, serves as a departure point for boats to the offshore islands of Pulau Rawa, Pulau Besar, Pulau Tioman and Pulau Aur. To the north and south of this coastal town are a number of fine beaches.

115
116
117

116, 117 The Johor Safari World with its 350-metre long roller coaster track and ankoles, one of the rare species of wildlife in its drive-in animal park.

118   119

118 Endau, a coastal town near the Johor-Pahang border. Straddling the border on the outskirts of the town is the proposed Endau-Rompin national park. The rainforest in this 84,000-hectare park is believed to be about 130 million years old. It houses the largest single population of the extremely rare and endangered Sumatran rhinoceros. It is also home to a wide range of unique flora and fauna. In 1985, a large-scale expedition comprising Malaysian scientists, nature-lovers and youths spent six months conducting an on-the-ground scientific survey of the proposed park. Among the discoveries recorded were the Musa Gracilis, a rare and delicate wild banana plant which produces only three inedible bananas per comb, green prawns and a small green frog with "blue blood".

119 Desaru or "The Village of Casuarinas" is situated on a 20-kilometre stretch of sandy beach at Tanjung Penawar on the south-east corner of Johor. Tucked away in lush jungles, cascading falls, grassy glades and natural lakes, this newly-developed holiday resort has three types of accommodation – the traditional Minangkabau– style chalets, medium – class Desaru Merlin and the luxurious Desaru View Hotel.

120

120 Oil palm estates are a common sight in Malaysia, especially in Johor and along the west coast of the peninsula. Malaysia is now the world's largest producer of palm oil products, contributing more than 60 per cent of the total world supply.

CHAPTER 2

Picturesque Malaysia

PAHANG DARUL MAKMUR — The Adventure Land

Pahang, the largest state in Peninsular Malaysia, has an area of about 36,000 square kilometres, much of which is still densely covered with tropical rainforest rich in timber, wildlife and flora. Its main river system, Sungei Pahang, is the longest river in the peninsula. The state's early inhabitants were believed to have first settled in the valleys of its two main tributaries – Sungei Tembeling and Sungei Jelai – as large number of Paleolithic relics had been unearthed here.

The state packs in a 4,300 square kilometre National Park that is the ultimate where hard-core, rugged adventures are concerned; three hill stations, one of which features the country's only casino-in-the-sky where for some people, a turn at the roulette wheel is high adventure; and get-away-from-it-all beaches where organized adventure is sedate and salutary.

At Taman Negara, the jungle is reputed to be more than 130 million years old – even older than those in the Congo or Amazon. The great big outdoors here are ideal for the energetic; shooting the rapids, swimming, fishing for carp, capturing wild animals on film, scaling limestone outcrops or hills, may be even attempting to reach Peninsular Malaysia's highest peak, Gunung Tahan.

The state's three hill resorts provide adventure of a different sort. Fraser's Hill, a few hours from Kuala Lumpur by road, is coolly comfortable with graystone English-style cottages and English gardens dotting the seven hills of the resort. Civilized recreation like sedate jungle walks, a 18-hole golf course, a visit to the waterfalls or Government Flower Nursery are the main attractions.

Cameron Highlands lies 1,829 metres above sea level on the Pahang-Perak border and is the vegetable centre of the country. The three towns of Ringlet, Tanah Rata and Brinchang are charmingly located and offer a variety of chalets and cottages in the English-style for visitors. Excellent tea is grown and produced here while the sub-temperate and temperate flowers (like roses, dahlia, fuchsias and chrysanthemums) as well as vegetables like spring cabbages, lettuces and tomatoes thrive to great size. Much of the fresh produce is transported and consumed in the lowland urban towns.

Genting Highlands, at 1,700 metres above sea level and just a short drive from Kuala Lumpur has gained local significance as a leisure centre. Activities such as ski-on-grass, bowling cable-car rides and golfing provide the resort an aura of felicity. This aura is enhanced by the surrounding landscapes of hills, valleys, trees and its lake, which when seen as nature intended are totally captivating.

An adventure into the mysterious past comes in the form of a trip to Tasik Chini (Lake Chini). Like Scotland's Loch Ness with its Nessie monster, Tasik Chini is rumoured to be the home of a monster that dates from pre-historic times and guards a sunken city beneath the cover of lotus flowers. Plans are being drawn up to develop this site into a Robinson Crusoe-style tourist stop.

The get-away-from-it-all beach resort begins with that of Teluk Chempedak just outside the state capital of Kuantan, which is also the largest town in the state. Kuantan is also an important port serving the East Coast states and a place to take in some local cultural colour and handicrafts.

About 47 kilometres north of Kuantan is the coastal village of Cherating, location of Asia's first Club Meditterranee. Malay-style timber buildings on concrete stilts and pitched roofs give the holiday village a local flavour while organized activities ensure the adventure of holidaying here is comfortable and fun.

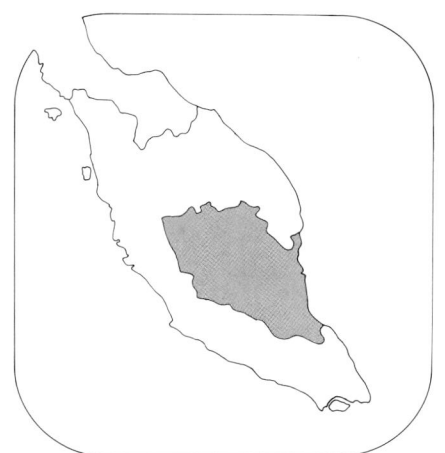

The country's lush tropical rainforest such as this in Pahang has existed virtually undisturbed for about 130 million years.

(continued from previous page)

Most famous of Pahang's beach resorts just has to be Pulau Tioman, an island paradise that's about 4 hours away from the little fishing port of Mersing by boat. Tioman's fame has been much celebrated, most memorably as the location for the fantasy island of Bali Hai in the movie version of Michener's "South Pacific". The island is fringed with sandy beaches, rich coral troves, a haven for big game fishing, for snorkelling and scuba diving. Jungle walks to observe the wild life or to reach the waterfalls can be an adventurous undertaking.

122 The Taman Negara (National Park) headquarters at Kuala Tahan is only accessible by river — a 60-kilometre journey up the Tembeling River from Kuala Tembeling. From the headquarters, numerous trails lead into the jungle which has more species of fauna and flora than anywhere else in the world.

123 124
125

123, 124 A variety of vegetation ranging from towering trees with interlacing branches to thick undergrowth characterizes Taman Negara, making it an ideal sanctuary for numerous species of fauna such as deer and spiders.

125 Travel within Taman Negara is mainly by rivers. Passengers are sometimes expected to get down from their boats and walk along the river bank at places where the river is either strewn with rocks or too shallow for boats to negotiate. The rivers, especially Sungei Tahan, are well-stocked with more than 300 species of fresh water fish such as the Kelasa (Scelero-pages Formosus) and the carp family, which includes the famous Mahseer of India, known locally as the Kelah. The Kelasa can frequently be seen leaping and "running" at very high speed at places where the water is deep and relatively calm while the Kelah prefer swifter reaches of the rivers.

126 **127**

126, 127 Nestling at 1,700 metres above sea level at the Pahang-Selangor border is Genting Highlands, Malaysia's latest and most exciting hill resort. Opened in 1971, this integrated hill resort has a cluster of modern hotels and a four-hectare artificial lake with a mini railway track circling it. Set amidst rolling hills about 700 metres from the resort centre is an 18-hole golf course. Linking the Sri Layang Hotel next to the golf course and the Genting Hotel at the resort proper is the country's longest cable-car system.

128 *(previous page)* At dawn, mists blanket many parts of Cameron Highlands, forming cotton-like integuments over rolling jungle-clad hills and valleys.

129 An *orang asli* village in Cameron Highlands. There are about 1,000 such villages throughout the peninsula. Whatever the *orang asli* cannot grow or obtain by hunting is supplied by the Government through the Orang Asli Affairs Department. The department is now trying to resettle villages in new sites with easier access to roads and urban areas. The *orang asli* are given land and encouraged to grow rubber trees and other cash crops.

130 Traditionally, most *orang asli* are either hunters or food gatherers. The man in the picture is holding a blow-pipe, the *orang asli*'s main hunting weapon. Strapped to their backs are aboriginal fishtraps made from bamboo and rattan obtained from the jungles.

131 To encourage the *orang asli* to send their children to schools, the Government provides free board and lodging for aboriginal children in urban schools. In bigger villages, the children attend schools near their homes.

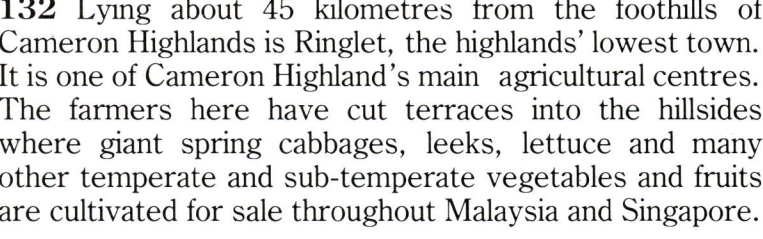

132

132 Lying about 45 kilometres from the foothills of Cameron Highlands is Ringlet, the highlands' lowest town. It is one of Cameron Highland's main agricultural centres. The farmers here have cut terraces into the hillsides where giant spring cabbages, leeks, lettuce and many other temperate and sub-temperate vegetables and fruits are cultivated for sale throughout Malaysia and Singapore.

133 The town of Tanah Rata has a number of Chinese restaurants and open-air stalls serving a variety of local food.

134 Tanah Rata is Cameron Highland's foremost town where there are a number of comfortable hotels and a variety of stores selling local produce like flowers, vegetables and fruits, including strawberries, and souvenirs such as aboriginal blow-pipes and shafts. A well-designed mountain resort, Tanah Rata has a number of jungle-walks leading to the Robinson Falls, Parit Falls, mountain peaks and other scenic spots. Cameron Highlands' most famous jungle walker was Jim Thompson, an American who founded the Thai silk industry after the Second World War. Thompson, who was holidaying in the highlands, left for a pre-dinner stroll on March 26, 1967 and has never been seen again.

135 Brinchang is the highest of Cameron Highlands' three towns. The road beyond this modest town leads to the Gunung Brinchang Wireless Station and smaller villages like Kampong Raja where a variety of vegetables and fruits is grown.

136 Lying just outside Ringlet is this man-made reservoir created by the Sultan Abu Bakar Dam for generating hydro-electricity. It supplies water through a 7.5-kilometre long tunnel to an underground power station which has a generating capacity of 100 megawatts. This 39.6-metre high composite structure consisting of three types of dams – rockfill, buttress and gravity – was completed in 1962.

137 Located beside a scenic lake near Ringlet is this cosy rest house called Foster's Lakehouse.

138 Ye Olde Smokehouse in Tanah Rata is a charming hotel, reminiscent of Swiss-style cottages.

139 The Merlin Hotel in Tanah Rata with an 18-hole golf course in front of it.

140 Nestling in the serene surroundings of Brinchang, Cameron Highlands' highest town, is the Sam Poh Wan Fatt Buddhist Temple.

137 138
139
140

141, 142 A luxuriant cover of vegetables of many varieties carpet the plateaus and terraces of Cameron Highlands. Vegetables ranging from cauliflower to rhubarb are harvested by the tons from these quadratic plots and later transported by lorries to be sold in urban areas in Malaysia and Singapore. Most of the farms are family-owned and work is shared out among everyone in the family. Even young children are seen sowing or reaping the harvest if they are not at school.

143 144
145

143 The cool climate in the Highlands makes it very ideal for growing flowers. There are numerous flower nurseries famous for their multi-chromatic flowers. Among the many varieties grown are chrysanthemums, roses, carnations, dahlias, fuchsias and "everlasting flowers". These much sought-after blooms are sent to all the main towns in West Malaysia and exported overseas.

144 Typifying many residents of Cameron Highlands, this Chinese girl is a picture of health and radiance.

145 This 100-year old rose tree growing in the Rose Garden Nursery in Brinchang no longer bears flowers.

146 *(following page)* Much of the cultivated land in Cameron Highlands such as this in the Sungei Palas estate owned by the Boh Tea Plantations is used for growing tea.

147 Tea bushes flourishing at Bharat Tea Plantation. The three-storey building on the slope of the hill is the plantation's factory where tea leaves are processed. At the factory, the leaves are spread in troughs where air is blown by powerful fans to dry them to about 50 per cent of the original moisture content. The flaccid leaves are then twisted and broken by machines in order to distort and rupture their internal cells and thus liberating their juices for fermentation. After the rolled leaves are sifted, they are sent for fermentation. The fermented leaves are then dried and converted to the familiar black tea leaves. The leaves are sorted into grades and then stored in bins to mature before they are finally packed.

148 The Boh Tea Plantation in Sungei Palas, Brinchang. About 2,035 hectares of the valley are under tea cultivation. The tea bushes have to be pruned to keep to working level and in prime condition *(brown area)*. The highest mountain in the Highland is the mist-shrouded Gunung Brinchang (2,018 metres high) and the famed Rose Gardens can be seen on the hill slopes *(left)* overlooking the tea valley.

149 *(following page)* Tea-pickers at the Sungei Palas Tea Valley. The young tea leaves are plucked every eleven or fifteen days. Total production of tea from the Boh Plantation at Sungei Palas is 580 tons per year.

149 150
151

150 Baskets filled with freshly-plucked tea leaves are carried to a nearby station to be weighed before they are sent to a factory for processing.

151 A tea collection station is a hive of activity as the tea-pickers bring their tea leaves to be weighed. An average picker manages about 40 kilogrammes of tea leaves in a day for which he or she is paid according to the weight of leaves picked.

152 Kuantan, the capital of Pahang, lies on the banks of the Kuantan River. This rapidly developing town is one of the biggest urban centres on the East Coast of Peninsular Malaysia. It is also an important port serving the East Coast states as well as a focal point of traditional Malay culture and authentic craftsmanship such as *batik* printing and *pandanus* leave weaving.

153 *(previous page)* The Hyatt *(with orange roof)* and the Merlin are Kuantan's premier hotels. Kuantan, with its famous beaches like Teluk Chempedak, is one of the East Coast's major seaside resorts.

154 Pulau Tioman is the largest of a group of 64 volcanic islands located in the South China Sea. It is accessible by boat from the fishing port of Mersing. From afar, the island resembles a giant figure reclining amidst the blue waters of the South China Sea. According to a local legend, the figure is that of an old woman known as "Nenek Si Mukut" who turned into a stone after a curse was cast on her. Fringed with sandy beaches and rich coral troves, Pulau Tioman's fame has been much celebrated, most memorably as the location for the fantasy island of Bali Hai in the Hollywood movie "South Pacific". This island, nominated by Geneva-based Magnum Press Agency as the world's most beautiful island at the "Beauty is synonymous in all islands" Festival for 1983/84, has a modern chalet-type hotel.

155 Resembling an emerald at 200 metres above sea level, this small uninhabited island off the Pahang Coast is Pulau Chebeh. Its clear blue water is a popular spot for scuba-diving, snorkelling and observation of rich marine life.

CHAPTER 2
Picturesque Malaysia

TERENGGANU — The Giant Turtle State

Beaches, beaches and yet more beaches, stretching for much of its 225-kilometre coastline are one of the outstanding features of this east coast state of Terengganu on Peninsular Malaysia. The South China Sea that washes the shore has always been a generous provider for the 600,000 people who live here. Fishing is the traditional occupation but lately with the discovery of off-shore oil deposits, the pace has quickened and lifestyle has begun to change.

One thing, though, has not changed for perhaps thousands of years. That is the annual pilgrimage from May to September of the giant leatherback turtles (Dermochelys Coriacea) which laboriously waddle up these famous beaches from their homes in the deep ocean to lay their eggs a hundred or more at a time. This mammoth turtle, a primitive fossil-animal dating back 100 million years or more, is toothless and has powerful forelimbs like large flippers. Its back has seven longitudinal ridges and a mosaic of small bones covered over by smooth, leathery skin. It weighs about half a ton and is almost 2.5 metres long.

Although the leatherback has been known to lay its eggs on South American shores, Malaysia is the home of one of the world's largest leatherback "nurseries" especially at Rantau Abang. The leatherback has long been coveted for its eggs. Its soft white eggs, the size of a ping pong ball are thought to have aphrodisiac qualities besides being a source of rich protein. More than a 100,000 eggs may be collected in one season. The female leatherback, after a single mating, can lay eggs for several more years and its life span can be over 100 years.

This leatherback is now an endangered species and conservation programmes have been implemented by the State Fisheries Department, the World Wild Life Fund Malaysia and the Malayan Nature Society to protect them from being extinct. Licensed egg collectors are required to sell back 10% of their harvest to the fisheries department for protected hatching and release into the sea. Before they are released, the baby turtles are tagged for record and scientific studies. The mortality rate of these baby turtles is high as birds, monitor lizards, dogs and sea predators will pick off these tiny offspring by the thousands as they take to the sea.

Why do the leatherbacks favour Rantau Abang beaches above others? According to Malay folklore, certain turtle-shaped rocks on the beaches there represent petrified leatherback ancestors; and the living leatherbacks return to these ancestral rocks to pay homage. But scientific studies suggest that the beaches at Rantau Abang have a very high rate of oxygen diffusion through the sand which is ideal for hatching as the embryos are still terrestrial in that they need to take in oxygen through the shell. If laid in water, they would perish. Turtle watching is a fascinating experience and each year this beach draws thousands of nocturnal visitors.

Another aspect of life in Terengganu that has remained unchanged is the penchant for flying giant-size kites in the shape of animals, birds and stylized objects. Not to be outdone in this state where turtles and kites come super-sized are spinning tops. Some larger than a dinner plate, these giant tops are definitely no child's play – only grown men with years of practice, skill and strength can make the tops hum and spin like a dream.

Likewise, it is often a man-sized operation when it comes to fashioning a typically graceful Terengganu boat, complete with a finely carved bow. Pride of

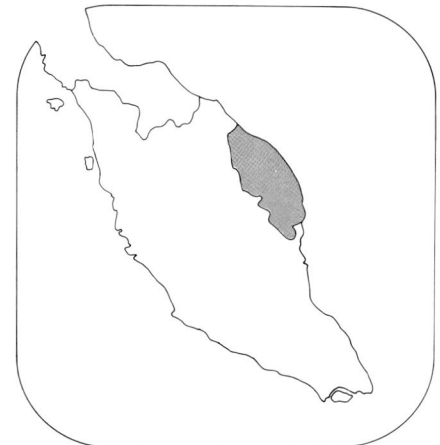

A leatherback turtle returning to the sea after laying its eggs on the beach of Rantau Abang. Every year, almost 300,000 people visit this famed beach to witness the annual pilgrimage of these giant leatherbacks. Besides the leatherbacks, other species such as the agar, lipas and the karas turtles also come to lay their eggs in Pulau Redang, Pulau Perhentian and Kijah in Kemaman.

(continued from previous page)

workmanship is definitely alive and well in these parts, seen not only in boat making but also in the brassware, the weaving of silk and *songket* fabrics and the mats from the leaves of the *pandanus* In fact, Terengganu's *songket* – fabric shot through with silver and gold threads – is justifiably one of the state's prized products.

Among its other treasures are those relating to the sea. Popular beaches at Marang, Teluk Mengkuang and Bukit Keluang, while off-shore coral islands like Pulau Kapas and Pulau Redang offer clear, calm water perfect for diving and observation of coral and marine life.

157 The coral island of Pulau Kapas is located just six kilometres from the fishing village of Marang. This uninhabited island is famous for its corals, seashells, sandy beaches and crystal-clear water. It can be reached in about half an hour by boat from Marang.

158, 159 Fishing is one of the main occupations of the East Coast inhabitants particularly those in Terengganu. The seas off the Terengganu coastline are rich fishing grounds providing for the many fisherfolk who live here. Some of the fish is salted and dried under the sun before being sold in sundry shops and market-places.

160 Kuala Terengganu, the state capital and royal town of Terengganu, lies on a promontory formed by the sea on one side and the wide Terengganu River on the other side. From a sleepy hollow, this East Coast town (which literally translated means Terengganu rivermouth) is now emerging as a rapidly developing urban centre partly as a result of the recent discovery of rich oil fields off the Terengganu coast. One major project is the proposed multi-million dollar bridge across the Terengganu River.

161 Pulau Karak *(foreground)* and Pulau Bidung Laut are two lush tropical islands located about 15 kilometres from Kampung Merang. Like Pulau Perhentian, the surrounding waters here are also noted for their rich marine life. For local fishermen, these two islands provide them shelter from storms during their fishing trips. Today, Pulau Bidung is off limit to them, as it is the temporary home of the "boat people" from Vietnam and Kampuchea before they are resettled in other countries.

162 Off-shore fishermen in Terengganu use the conventional *pukat hanyut* or dragnet method to catch their fish. The government is currently providing modern technology and subsidies to encourage the fishermen to engage in deep-sea fishing.

163 Pulau Perhentian Kecil, the smaller of the two Perhentian islands, lies about 21 kilometres off the Terengganu coast. This coral island is famous for its crystal clear waters and coral beds rich in marine life. It is also home to about 1,000 families whose main occupation is fishing.

161 162
163

164, 166 The Tanjung Jara beach is part of Terengganu's 225 kilometres of soft, sandy beaches stretching from Besut in the north to Kemaman in the south. The idyllic beach set against a backdrop of natural forests ends at a rocky point studded with boulders.

165 A chalet at the Tanjong Jara Beach Resort, about 55 kilometres from Kuala Terengganu. Set in a palm fringed lagoon, the resort has a number of chalets lying in a self-contained village setting. Designed in the traditional manner, the chalets are made from wood skilfully carved by Terengganu's master craftsmen.

CHAPTER 2
Picturesque Malaysia

KELANTAN — The Handicraft State

If there is one element that characterizes this border state of Kelantan, it must be its people's highly-developed handicraft skills. From wood carving a palace down to the gossamer delicacy of its renowned filigree silver jewellery, the Kelantanese who number just about a million, have no peers.

Simple people who have no need for the rough and tumble of urbanized living, the average Kelantanese is either a farmer or a fisherman with deep reverence for his culture and traditions. So it is that his leisure pursuits are often centuries old – flying the incredibly large kites (sometimes 2.4 metres in wingspan, as long as 1.8 metres) called *wau*; spinning giant tops; or enjoying the unique Kelantanese dance-drama, the *mak yong* which began as a court diversion; sitting night after night listening to the stories of the Ramayana recounted with the aid of shadow play puppets *(wayang kulit)*. In every instance of these pastimes, the inescapable fact is that the design of the kites, the smoothness of the tops, the costumes of the *mak yong*, the puppets of the shadow play reflect the innate craftsmanship of their makers.

For export, the people fashion infinitely fine silverware from tea sets to tiny lapel pins– which have won the state much fame around the world. The most skilled of these silver-smiths are found in Kampong Sireh, a suburb of Kota Baharu, the state capital. *Kain songket* weaving and deft transformation of dried *pandanus* into mats, bags or hats are chiefly women's while woodcarving, leatherworking and working with brass tend to be men's work. However the labour is divided, all of these handicrafts bear the stamp of that special Kelantanese care and skill.

As it is primarily a rural economy, Kelantan's attractions tend to the tranquil. In Kota Baharu, the singular sight of women who dominate the buying and selling in the central market has often been remarked upon. Shrewd, hardworking queens of commerce, they lend a festive air to the place with their colourful clothes. A second sight worth taking in is the historic palace built in 1844 called Istana Besar, the preferred venue for royal functions like weddings or investiture. The palace with its elaborately etched wooden panels is a fine example of the people's carving skills.

North of Kota Baharu about 10 kilometres away is the evocatively-named Beach of Passionate Love or 'Pantai Cinta Berahi'. The soft, white sand, the fringe of casuarinas could perhaps have been responsible for its romantic naming. But however it originated, the beach has other rivals in the form of Pantai Irama (Melody Beach), Pantai Dalam Rhu (Beach in the Casuarinas) and Pantai Dasar Sabak.

Inland from the coast, near the town of Pasir Putih, Kelantan offers visitors the waterfalls of Jeram Pasu, Jeram Tapah and Cherang Tuli. The lake of Tok' Uban is a quiet alternative to the noisy falls and is a favourite with anglers hoping to nab a few freshwater fish. Deeper into the jungles of the Main Range is the home of a variety of wild life such as deer, *seladang* (wild buffaloes) and elephants, especially in the district of Ulu Kelantan where there are several salt-licks.

The culture, the handicrafts, the unhurried pace, the lure of absolute peace on beautiful beaches all go towards making Kelantan the perfect antidote for the over-civilized.

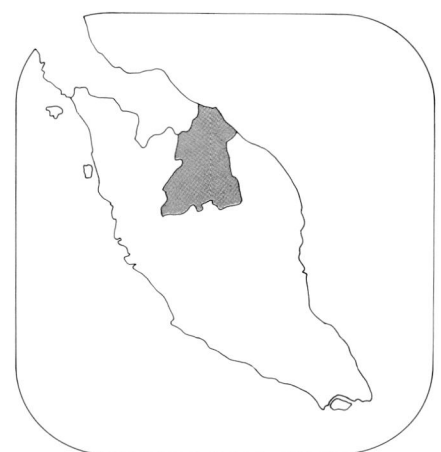

To the uninitiated, kite-flying is child's play. But in the East Coast of Peninsular Malaysia, especially Kelantan, it is taken seriously by adults. Kelantanese men take great pride in making and flying their own wau or giant kites which are often decorated with intricate Malay designs. The kites are very colourful and come in various shapes and sizes. The Wau Bulan (Moon Kite), for example, has a two-and-a-half metre wing span and measures three metres from head to tail. It has a concave-convex shape and flies the highest, reaching a height of about 460 metres.

168 Kota Baharu, the state capital and royal town of Kelantan, lies on the banks of the Kelantan River. It was once a thriving river-port but its importance has since declined due to the silted up rivermouth and the huge meanders.

169 *(following page)* Many of the traders at the central market in Kota Baharu are women. Sitting behind their produce ranging from fresh vegetables and fruits to colourful *batik* cloth and skilfully-woven bamboo baskets, these female traders, many of them chewing *sirih* or betel leaves, command great respect in the local business circle as they good-naturedly strike a bargain, often to their advantage.

171   172   173

170 *(previous page)* A *rebana* is a traditional Malay drum made from a hollowed-out log. It is an important musical instrument used for competition and recreation and also as accompaniment during ceremonial rites. *Rebana* competitions are usually held at the end of each harvesting season. Judges award points on timing, rhythm, tone and style of each player.

171 *Silat*, the Malay art of self-defence, was at one time an essential part of a young man's education. This art, believed to have been introduced to Melaka by a North Sumatran religious teacher in the early fifteenth century, is a popular pursuit in Kelantan. Students are taught by their *guru* (teacher) to parry any attack by opponents armed with a *keris* (a double-edged dagger) or a sword. *Silat*, accompanied by rhythmic beats of gongs and drums, is usually performed during weddings and special ceremonies.

172, 173 Top-spinning is a favourite pastime amongst the East Coast Malays, especially those in Kelantan. The giant tops *(gasing)* are fashioned out of selected local hardwoods. There are many types of giant tops, the bigger ones rimmed with steel and weighing up to 5.5 kilogrammes. Top-spinning requires great skills. After a top is launched, it is quickly scooped off the ground with a thin wooden bat and then transferred onto a metal receptacle on a short wooden post. An expert player can make his top spin for as long as two hours. Top-spinning competitions are held every Wednesday and Saturday afternoon (except during the Muslim fasting month) at the Gelanggang Seni, the state's cultural centre in Kota Baharu. Besides the Gelanggang Seni, competitions are also held in villages during the period when the paddy is ripening and according to legend, tops could then bring good harvests.

175
174 176

174 The greater part of *mak yong* performances is accompanied by an orchestra comprising a three-stringed *rebab* (viol), two double-ended cylindrical *gendang* (drums) and a pair of signal *tawak-tawak* (gongs). Seen here is a musician playing the Malay oboe when the longest of the *mak yong* dances, *tari ragam*, is performed.

175 The *mak yong* is another dance drama with elements of opera and comedy. Originally a favourite of Malay rulers of the northern states of the peninsula, the *mak yong* is now performed in the East Coast states, especially Kelantan. The 16-member troupe of performers, usually teenage girls selected for their beauty and ability to dance, sing and act, recount tales full of action, romance, humour and magic. In Kelantan, the *mak yong* is usually performed during special occassions like the Puja Umur celebrating the birthday of the Sultan of Kelantan.

176 One of the main characters in the *mak yong* is Pakyong Tua (Older Prince), who is either the father or future father-in-law of Pakyong Muda (Young Prince).

177 *Wayang kulit* (shadow play) is one of Kelantan's most popular cultural pursuits. There are two forms of *wayang kulit* – Wayang Siam and Wayang Melayu (Jäwa) – both based on the great Hindu epics of Ramayana and Mahabharatha. The puppet figures carved from buffalo hides and fitted with long handles are skilfully manipulated by a Tok Dalang (Father of the Mysteries) behind a canvas screen. The shadows are cast onto the screen with the help of an oil lamp or an electric bulb. *Wayang kulit* is usually staged at weddings, births, rice harvests and other auspicious occasions.

177

178   180
179

178, 180 Although Kelantanese are predominantly Muslims, the state also has a number of Buddhist temples due to its proximity to Thailand. The most famous is Wat Phothivihan in the village of Kampung Jambu, about 11 kilometres from Kota Baharu. The temple's reclining Buddha, which measures 40 metres long, nine metres wide and 11 metres high, is reputed to be the largest in South-East Asia.

179 *Menora* is seen only in Kelantan. This dance-drama, which is believed to have developed in Thailand about 2,000 years ago, was introduced to Kelantan during the second half of the nineteenth century. It is performed by an all-male cast who also assume female roles. Adventures dating from ancient folkfore are enacted by slow rhythmic movements of legs, arms and fingers. An orchestra of drums, gongs, scrape instruments and the *serunai*, a Malay oboe, provides the music. It is usually performed during special occassions such as the Puja Umur celebrations.

CHAPTER 2
Picturesque Malaysia

SARAWAK — The Nature State

Mention longhouse, *tuak* (a traditional rice wine) or hornbill to almost any Malaysian and the association is instantly with Sarawak. But this land of rivers, largest of the Malaysian states at 124,450 square kilometres covering the north-west portion of Borneo Island, is many more things than these three.

Sarawak is nature, at its most rugged and primitive. Rivers in the state are often fast-moving with treacherous rapids being fairly commonplace. The Sungei Rejang is the longest river in Malaysia. Limestone outcrops are larger than life, craggier than most and more cavernous than those encountered elsewhere. In the Gunung Mulu National Park (it is one of six – the others being Bako, Niah, Samunsan, Similajau and Lambir Hills) there are limestone outcrops that stretch for 40 kilometres. Right beneath these peaks are networks of caves including the world's largest, the Sarawak Chamber and the Deer Cave – the longest cave passage known to man. The Niah Caves in the Niah National Park are also no ordinary pile of limestone. Here, the bones of the first South-East Asian man dated to about 40,000 years were discovered.

Sarawak is also a naturalist's haven. Aptly called the "Land of the Hornbills", the state is renowned for its attractive hornbills. Another red letter day for naturalists is the once-a-year Open Day at the forbidden island of Talang-Talang. Sometime in June or July, this island sanctuary of the giant green turtles is thrown open to the public. Near Talang-Talang are some remarkable islands, the Satang Besar, Satang Kecil, Sempadi and Lakei.

Sarawak is also history. In the early period, Sarawak was ruled by the Brooke family of "White Rajahs". The Saga of the "White Rajahs" rule ended with the arrival of the Japanese during the Second World War. Sarawak was handed over to the British and remained under British rule when Malaya obtained its independence in 1957. It was only in 1963 that Sarawak together with Sabah joined the Federation to form Malaysia. The rule of the "White Rajah" is memorably recorded in two locations. In Kuching, the state capital, stands the Istana built in 1870 by Raja Charles Brooke and the Sarawak Museum built in 1891, both speak of the colonial era, while ancient temples and artefacts in the latter speak of a rich cultural heritage. A mere hour's express boat ride from Kuching is Santubong's fishing village and the popular Damai Beach Resort, the second repository of Sarawak's past. The village was once an important trading partner of China during the Tang and Sung dynasties which spanned from the 7th to the 13th Century A.D. Around the village are even more evidences of overseas contact: Hindu and Buddhist rock carvings have been discovered at many archaeological sites.

Sarawak is also colourful ethnic communities and unique traditional festivals. Travel up the Skrang River puts one in touch with the Iban longhouses, for here in the upper reaches are many of these villages of the indigenous people. The Ibans account for about 30% of the population in Sarawak. They are largely located in the Second and Third Divisions. The Bidayuh are found mostly in the inland areas of South-Western Sarawak in the First Division. Their longhouses and cultures are similar to the Ibans but their languages and customs differ. The Muruts and their relatives the Kelabits are found in the Fourth and Fifth Division whereas the Punans are generally a normadic group. For unique festivals, the annual Gawai Dayak festival held in June to mark the end of the rice harvest must surely be the ultimate. Prayers are offered for the new season and then the fun begins: the *ngajat* or Dayak Warrior Dance, blow-pipe demonstrations and cock fights.

Sarawak's nickname "Land of the Hornbills" is derived from this bulky omnivorous bird found in the state's tropical jungles. This arboreal bird has a plumage which is predominantly black and has an enormous bill usually surmounted with a horny casque.

182 Perched on the banks of the Sarawak River is Kuching, the capital and administrative and financial centre of Sarawak. This riverine town is the home of the world-famous Sarawak Museum, which houses the state's archaeological and cultural artefacts including a fine collection of tribal weapons.

183 Wisma Saberkas, the headquarters of the Sarawak United National Youth Organization, overlooks the Sarawak River. This imposing 19-storey complex is one of Kuching's most prominent landmarks.

185

184 Bintulu, is one of Sarawak's fastest growing urban centres. Among the numerous projects presently being undertaken here are a new international airport (*left*), a multi-billion ringgit gas project, a deepwater port and residential suburbs to cater for the sudden influx of migrants from other parts of the state.

185 Miri, situated near the Sarawak-Brunei border, is a boom town whose wealth is largely derived from its vast oil resources. Much of this coastal town is now being redeveloped.

186 187

186 The Deer Cave is one of the newly discovered gigantic caverns hidden underneath Gunung Mulu. Compared to the other caves, the Deer Cave is relatively easy to reach and has been explored many times by spelaeologists.

187 The forested mountains of Gunung Mulu in the Gunung Mulu National Park with the entrance to Deer Cave on the right.

188 *(following page)* "Rubic Tubes" in Cobweb Cave. The Cobweb Cave contains a giant network of interlinked passages and galleries. A Malaysian-British team sponsored by the Malaysian Airlines System in 1984 succeeded in exploring about 14 kilometres of this cave to where it reaches Terikan River, some 1,200 metres below ground level. Certain cave walls here are white and enamel-smooth, scraped clean by swifts. On the floor, the spelaeologists found the skeletons of millions of tiny animals whose species are yet unspecified. The high points of the cave are shrouded in mist while the lowest places are completely dry.

188 190 191
189

189 The Valley of the Shadow of Hanging Death, Benaret Caverns. Many of the caves in Gunung Mulu are strewn with huge boulders.

190 The reward for hours of squeezing, crawling, climbing and swimming your way into the dark maze beneath the forested mountains of the Gunung Mulu National Park is the privilege to behold the magnificent Sarawak Chamber, the world's largest cavern and also the biggest enclosed space of any kind. With a staggering volume of between 10 to 12 million cubic metres, the Sarawak Chamber can hold 40 Jumbo jets with room to spare. According to a London's Royal Geographical Society (RGS) team which discovered the cavern in 1980, the cave is three times as big as the world's previously largest cave, La Verns in France.

191 The river passage of Clearwater Cave, the longest cave in South-East Asia. So far, about 62 kilometres of this cave have been explored. The cave contains some of the world's finest underground rivers.

192 Located in the centre of the Niah National Park is Niah Caves, one of the world's largest caverns. Here, archaeologists have found evidence of man's existence from as early as 40,000 years ago. One of the caves known as the "Painted Cave" was once used as a burial ground. Rock paintings found in this cave resemble boats used as coffins. The Niah Caves are also the home of millions of three species of swiftlets and twelve species of bats. The nests of the swiftlets are used in preparing bird's nest soup, a prized Chinese delicacy. The long bamboo pole on the left is used by workers to reach the bird nests which are usually found in crevices in the roofs of the caves. Another commercial activity carried out in these caves is the collection of guano, the excrement of birds and bats which is used as fertiliser.

193 Shooting the rapids at Wong Silau, Sungei Ngemah, a tributary of Batang Rejang. Much of Sarawak's internal transportation system uses its vast network of navigable waterworks.

194 An Iban longhouse at Long Senyut in Sarawak's remote Seventh Division. Usually built of wood, bamboo and attap propped high up on stilts, longhouses vary greatly in sizes, housing any number between 4 to 100 families. The interior is divided into many units, each occupied by a family. Each unit has a bedroom and a kitchen and opens out into a *ruai* or large common verandah where residents gather for social activities and important functions such as weddings, funerals and feasting. Guests are entertained here before they are taken inside the living quarters.

195 A night scene at a longhouse in Punan Busang. The tribal man is playing a traditional harp to provide music for the *ngajat* (a Dayak warrior dance). The harp is hand-made from the wood of a soft tree found in the Sarawak jungles.

196 An Iban man from the Sungei Bunuk longhouse beside the Skrang River all ready to perform the *ngajat,* a Dayak warrior dance usually performed during the Gawai Dayak festival to mark the end of the rich harvest. The feathers on the man's headgear are obtained from a hornbill.

194 195
196

197 A pretty Sarawakian lady dressed in a colourful traditional costume during the Gawai Dayak festival to mark the end of the rice harvest. Sarawak's indigenous people are very artistic as evidenced by their skilfully-made costumes and headgears.

198 An Iban boy enjoying a comfortable ride in a special basket strapped to his mother's back.

199 The Muruts are found in both Sarawak and Sabah. In Sarawak, these indigenous people are known as Tagals. They and their relatives, the Kelabits, live in longhouses in the Fourth and Fifth Divisions. In Sabah, the Muruts are found along the upper reaches of the Padas River and near the Indonesian and Sarawak borders. There are language differences between the Muruts of Sarawak and those in Sabah. Basically a hospitable and generous people, the Muruts like to dance and sing. Their livelihood is largely dependent on shifting cultivation and hunting.

197 198
199

CHAPTER 2
Picturesque Malaysia

SABAH — The Mount Kinabalu State

No other single feature so dominates this state on the north-west of Borneo island as Mount Kinabalu, that granite peak soaring 4,101 metres to become South-East Asia's highest mountain.

The peak, which is heavily shrouded in mists many days in a year, is as thickly covered in legend and folklore as well. Some relate to the origin of its name, putting forth that it is a corrupted form that meant "the Chinaman's place". Others, like the Kadazans, Sabah's largest group of indigenous people, simply hold the mountain sacred. As for die-hard adventurers, the mountain by just being there, offers a rare challenge to be conquered.

Challenge aside, the peak is the focal point of the Kinabalu National Park in which masses of orchids of more than 800 species and 500 species of birds can be observed. Here too, if fortune smiles, the world's largest flower, the one-metre wide Rafflesia could unfold before your eyes. Also in the park near Ranau are the Poring hot springs, bubbling and steaming with sulphurous fumes. The distinctive call of the hornbill can sometimes be heard as a flock swoops through the Poring rain forest. Mynah birds, barking deer, grey monkeys and the rare Sumatran rhinoceroses are also inhabitants of the forest.

While animals reign in these forests, the people keep mostly to the coastal areas. Three quarters of the 1.1 million stay there despite the state's sprawling size of 72,500 square kilometres.

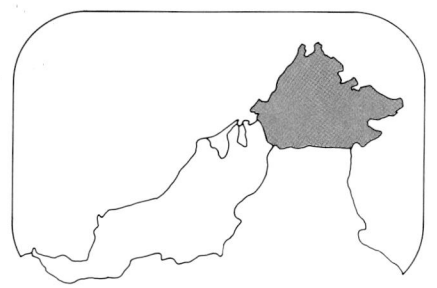

A morning view of Mount Kinabalu from the Kinabalu National Park headquarters.

The state capital of Kota Kinabalu is relatively new, built as it is on the ruins of the original town of Jesselton which was razed during the Second World War. Sited on Gaya Bay, the town is just north of its own premier beach resort, Tanjung Aru. Across the bay lies Tunku Abdul Rahman National Park with its five islands of Gaya, Sapi, Mamutik, Sulug and Manukan – a haven of coral life, tropical fish and deserted beaches. Prince Philip Park is the other recreational centre adjacent to Kota Kinabalu. Besides satisfying the need for inner peace, the park, with its host of stalls selling a wide range of local delicacies, also gratifies the inner man.

Further north about 77 kilometres away is Kota Belud, a Bajau town on the slopes of the Crocker Range. The Bajau, expert horsemen who wheel and turn with speed, gather in the town every Sunday morning for their *tamu* or open-air markets. Under a clear blue sky, trade is brisk as the rural folk sell everything from cattle to tobacco, fresh fruits and vegetables to betel nut.

Two other towns bear description. One is Labuan, recently designated the second Federal Territory of Malaysia, an island just made for swimming and scuba diving.

The other is Sandakan, 400 kilometres from Kota Kinabalu and a booming centre for the state's timber industry. It was once the capital of North Borneo and was completely destroyed during Second World War and then re-built. For naturalists, its appeal comes from its proximity to Sepilok Sanctuary, the world's largest orang utan rehabilitation centre. In this centre, special attention is paid to young stranded or orphaned orang utan. They are taught with love and patience so that they can, once again over time, regain the instincts of survival – instincts lost through overdependence on man. For entrepreneurs, it is the Gomantong Caves across Sandakan Bay, source of edible birds' nests made by the swiflets in the roofs of the caves.

Sabah, approximately 78% of which is still under evergreen rainforest and blessed with natural deep harbours and a variety of tourist attractions, is more than "The Land Below the Wind". It is a rare instance of a land of great opportunity.

201
202 203

201 Kota Kinabalu's most prominent landmark is undoubtedly the 31-storey Sabah Foundation building. This cylindrical, mirror-fronted building has a revolving restaurant and ministerial suites.

202 A unique community of Sabah is the "sea hermits" who live in little boats that float on the waters surrounding the state's many off-shore islands.

203 Tanjung Aru Beach Resort, Sabah's premier playground by the sea, with Kota Kinabalu, the state capital, in the distance. Kota Kinabalu, lying on Gaya Bay with its deep archorage, is a relatively new town erected on the ruins of the original town of Jesselton which was razed during the Second World War. Built to replace Sandakan as the state capital, Kota Kinabalu has grown from a small coastal trading post to a thriving cosmopolitan centre. Located across the bay is a cluster of islands gazetted as the Tunku Abdul Rahman National Park, a sanctuary for numerous species of corals and tropical fish.

204 Sandakan, the former capital of North Borneo, lies on a bay along the north-eastern coast of Sabah. It is one of the state's major commercial centres. Products from its hinterland such as timber, rattan, copra, palm oil and bird's nests from the nearby Gomantong Caves are brought and loaded onto boats for export. Situated on the outskirts of the town is Sepilok Sanctuary, the world's largest *orang utan* park.

205 A stilt village off the coast of Semporna, a small town on the south-eastern tip of Sabah. The residents here are fishermen and they lead a simple life.

206 A cultured pearl farm at Pulau Bohey Dulang, a small island off the coast of Semporna.

207 Malaysian climbers taking a short break at Sayat-Sayat camp (3,906 metres) on the slope of Mount Kinabalu after conquering Low's Peak. The Kinabalu National Park Authority awards first class certificates to climbers who have conquered Low's Peak and second class certificates to those who have reached Sayat-Sayat.

208 This unusual gigantic rock formation sculptured by the forces of nature stands out majestically in Low's Gully, Mount Kinabalu. This half-bestial, half-fowl rock can be seen from Low's Peak, the summit of Mount Kinabalu.

207 208

209 *(previous page)* Mount Kinabalu, Malaysia's highest mountain, dominates Sabah's pristine landscape. The Kadazans, Sabah's largest indigenous group, call the mountain "Akinabalu" meaning the home of departed spirits. Despite its immense size, Mount Kinabalu is a relatively young mountain. Its origins date back nine million years when a solidified core of volcanic rock began swelling up from the depths below, pushing its way through the overlying rocks. It is believed that this upward movement is still taking place. According to a team of Japanese geologists, the mountain is estimated to grow at a rate of about five millimetres every year. At one time, glaciers used to cover much of the mountain. Today, ice can sometimes be found in the rock pools near the summit.

210 Another majestic wind-swept peak on top of Mount Kinabalu.

211 Donkey Ears, a unique rock formation that serves as a beacon guiding mountaineers to the summit of Mount Kinabalu.

The Federal Territory of LABUAN

212 Lying about 128 kilometres to the south-west of Kota Kinabalu is the island of Labuan, gazetted as Malaysia's second Federal Territory in 1985. Separated from Sabah by a narrow 8-kilometre channel, Labuan is the country's only free port. It is renowned as a diamond and sapphire centre. A memorial here marks the place where the Japanese forces in North Borneo surrendered at the end of the Second World War.

CHAPTER 3

Kuala Lumpur – minarets of old, visions of new

One of the first things that strikes a newcomer to Malaysia's capital city, Kuala Lumpur, is that it is not any one single shaping spirit or symbol that dominates it. It is not a copy of Manhattan, bristling with skyscrapers lining arrow-straight avenues and streets – although Kuala Lumpur has its share of towering highrises. Neither is it an echo of Paris with the elegant Champs Elysee – despite the forest park at Bukit Nanas and the Lake Gardens the city boasts of. Nor is Kuala Lumpur ancient with castles brooding over the River Thames – even though an old mosque serenely presides on a tongue of land at the point where two rivers mingle, the spot from which the city had its beginning.

Instead, Kuala Lumpur is a marvellous mix where minarets of old jauntily co-exist with multi-storey slabs of glass and marble; where the city life is made richer by the intermingling of four main cultures; where entrepreneurs and political leaders share a common vision of building a more vibrant and robust country.

Yet a mere hundred years or so ago, this thriving metropolis was nothing but a swamp land. In 1857, a group of 87 prospectors poled their way up to the confluence of the Kelang and Gombak Rivers in search of tin. It was to cost them dearly for within the first month, 70 were dead from fever. The survivors however, succeeded in their quest and soon more miners joined them, opening up more tin mines. Settlers and traders quickly followed in their wake, building homes and trading posts until by 1870, the population numbered 2,000. Apropos of the location (which is marked today by the Masjid Jamek on the tongue of land abutting the confluence), the settlement was named "Kuala Lumpur" which means muddy confluence.

The early years were hardly smooth sailing for the inhabitants. Like many other frontier towns, bloody gang wars, murders, fires and epidemics took their toll. It was into this cauldron of seething iniquity that Yap Ah Loy (the famed Chinese Kapitan or Headman), Frank Swettenham (the first British Resident) and Tengku Kudin (a Kedah prince who was the son-in-law of Sultan Abdul Samad, the Ruler of Selangor then) ventured, imposing and maintaining law and order. By the 1880s, the prosperous little township received another fillip when tin prices soared which in turn created a rich middle class. With their new-found wealth, these early tycoons built magnificent mansions along Jalan Ampang which remain today an exclusive enclave.

Kuala Lumpur by 1896 replaced Kelang as the State capital and was already cosmopolitan in its population mix: the 30,000 inhabitants comprised the indigenous Malays, Chinese tin miners and traders, Indians whom the British had brought to the peninsula to construct roads, railways and as employees in the civil service.

Despite the many examples of racially-mixed residential neighbourhoods in and around the City, ethnic quarters remain as hangovers from this earlier period. Kampong Baru with its wooden houses, mosque and *suraus* is an urban kampung still hanging on to its rural Malay lifestyle. Chinatown in the older section of the City remains outwardly unchanged with its clan houses and push-stalls lining the narrow roads hawking all manner of fruits, clothes and the deep-red roast "Pudu ducks". A "Little India" is easily recognized in sections of the City like Sentul or Brickfields by their colourful temples with deities, banana leaf restaurants and the wafts of heavily scented flowers from the garland makers.

Another legacy to the City from the days of Swettenham, Yap Ah Loy and Tengku Kudin is its single-minded growth. But it is a vision of growth that prudently takes into consideration the City's past.

A 1937 picture of Kuala Lumpur with the (Royal) Selangor Club building and its historic field in the centre. In the vicinity are some of the city's earliest major buildings. Among them are the State Secretariat (now the Sultan Abdul Samad building), the General Post Office, the Public Works Department and the (Standard) Chartered Bank buildings.

So it is that those seemingly airy confections, the minarets atop the Moorish-style Railway Station, still get the full tourist treatment as a "must-see" alongside the stunning white edifice with lacey frills, the Dayabumi Complex. Likewise the imposing Sultan Abdul Samad Building with its copper domes and famous clock tower; the Padang opposite on which sprawls the English Tudor-style Royal Selangor Club; the National Art Gallery which was once the Majestic Hotel; the Le Coq D'Or restaurant made over from the original palatial home of Chua Cheng Bok; and the Central Market now undergoing a new lease of life as renovations are being made to make it a version of London's Covent Garden – all of them fine examples of a bygone era but lovingly maintained as integral parts of the overall whole that is Kuala Lumpur.

Superimposed over these concrete statements of the past, yet never crowding them out, are visions of the new that are helping to make this City of over a million people a force to be reckoned with on the international scene.

Architecturally, the new high-rises and shopping complexes are far from sterile repetitions seen in any large city. The desire to inject a Malaysian identity to the buildings while conforming to the rules of form and function probably had a big hand in ensuring the City avoided becoming a mini – Manhattan. Instead, graceful marvels like the LUTH building – its shape inspired by the *rebana,* a traditional Malay drum – give the skyline greater interest. Other designers have chosen to re-interpret the traditional Minangkabau roofs with their distinctive sweeping points, blending them with the modern upward thrust of the high-rises. The overall impression, then, is a skyline of interesting variety and one where old and new somehow balance, counterpoint and complement each other.

This seemingly odd pairing of past and present continues in the way Kuala Lumpur people live. It is not unusual to see a top-level executive, perhaps a habitue of one of the many exclusive clubs or discos like Regine's, round off his evening in an unlikely setting: hunkering down to a bowl of soup or noodles at some favourite night stall. Or to spy the modern housewife who is quite at home shopping in the busy supermarkets. Neither is it incongruous to see a girl in traditional *baju kurung* one moment, then in the next in leotards at a gymnasium or sweating it out in some aerobic class. And while many a gleaming BMW or Mercedes Benz may hare down the super six-lane highways to keep an urgent business appointment, perhaps just as many bicycles and a few trishaws throng the narrow streets quietly going about their tasks.

While the past 100 years have contributed to the flowering of the City into an important commercial and financial centre, it is rightly the present and the future that preoccupy planners and businessmen.

So far, the City has a wide array of luxury hotels, restaurants, discos, night clubs and pubs for those in search of diversion. For leisure and entertainment of a different complexion, there are cinemas, amusement arcades, parks, sports centres and concert halls. The businessman is well catered for as well because foreign and local banks abound in the City. And with the opening of the Putra World Trade Centre, acclaimed as one of the largest and most sophisticated of world trade centres, his need for a super convention site has been met.

For the future, more is in store as a natural development of the vital step taken in 1974 when the City was made Federal Territory occupying 244 square kilometres. The next milestone was the formation of the Federal Territory Ministry in 1978 to plan and develop the nation's premier city.

An aspect of the City's future reiterates the "old beside the new". A number of the older, recognized landmarks have been gazetted as historic buildings worthy of preservation and more are earmarked by the Heritage of Malaysia Trust. On the flipside and curiously not at all at odds with this concern with preservation is the development carried out by the Urban Development Authority. The City's "Golden Triangle" is currently being monitored and studied for redevelopment, a projected renaissance of the area being the target. Under this plan, shophouses past their prime would make way for modern multi-storey, multi-functional offices and shopping complexes so that potential businesses unable to acquire space in the crowded commercial base of Petaling Street and Jalan Tuanku Abdul Rahman can relocate here.

Another plan that will have future ramifications for the City is the recent Structural Plan prepared by City Hall. In additional to the big picture of the City's growth directions, it sets out the crucial proposed development of the Light Rail Transit (LRT) system and Aerobus Project. Both are aimed at dispersing traffic from congested City streets while providing faster and more efficient travel for a population that is expected to grow by leaps and bounds.

To go from a clutch of trading posts to a modern metropolis, from 2,000 people to over a million in the period of about 100 years is achievement indeed. But the next 100 years probably hold the bigger challenge. Given a Kuala Lumpur where its people have demonstrated a talent for reaching out to visions of the new while one foot remains firmly planted in its heritage, it is likely to be a future balanced, steady and with all signs of life intact.

(previous page) The confluence of Sungei Gombak and the Sungei Kelang – the birth place of the city more than 100 years ago. In the foreground is the Moorish-style Sultan Abdul Samad building while the city's oldest mosque, Masjid Jamek, is located on the tongue of land bounded by the two rivers. These two buildings have been extensively renovated to their present grandeur.

214 Modern high-rise buildings such as the Apera ULG, MAS, Promet and Shangri-La Hotel dominate the skyline in this highly-developed sector of the city. In the foreground is Jalan Raja Chulan with Jalan P. Ramlee on the left and Jalan Sultan Ismail on the right. The sprawling greenery on the right is the Selangor Turf Club Race Course. The race course will soon be moved to another site outside the city while the vacated area will be developed into a public park. The two white buildings at the far end of the race course are the LUTH (Pilgrims' Management and Fund Board) and PNB (Permodalan Nasional Bhd) buildings. The 38-storey LUTH building has a vertical curvature design – a simple circular edifice which tapers at the centre. It is one of the few buildings in the world with such a design.

215 *(following page)* Urban re-development, a process whereby old buildings are demolished and replaced by modern high-rise buildings, is going on at a fast pace in the heart of the city. As a result of this re-development process, which is under the control of the Urban Development Authority (UDA), scores of modern edifices such as the Dayabumi complex and the Bukit Aman Police Headquarters now grace the city's skyline. Under construction on top of Court Hill is the Malayan Banking headquarters building. To make way for this massive project, the city's lower courts buildings, formerly located on this hill, were demolished and new ones built on the outskirts of the city. Despite her rapid development, the heart of the city still retains pockets of lush greenery. One such area is the Bukit Nanas Forest Reserve in the foreground. Rising 225 metres above sea-level, this forest reserve has several foot-paths to enable visitors to have a glimpse of a typical Malaysian tropical rainforest.

216 Standing on a hillock set in rich parkland near the Lake Gardens is the Parliament House, the symbol of democracy in Malaysia. Dominating the complex is an 18-storey office tower. The House of Representatives and the Senate are housed in a three-storey block next to it.

217 Overlooking the Parliament House at the northern end of the Lake Gardens is the National Monument. Designed by Felix de Weldon, the creator of the famed Iwo Jiwa Memorial in Washington, this massive bronze structure was constructed in 1960 to commemorate members of the country's security forces who died in action against communist terrorists during the country's 12-year Emergency (1948-1960). Behind the bronze structure is a cenotaph, a monument to those who died in the cause of peace and freedom during the two World Wars.

218 The magnificent white Moorish architecture building with domes, minarets, towers and arches is the Kuala Lumpur Railway Station built in 1911. Across the building is the Malayan Railway Administration Building. The National Mosque is also located prominently here – next to it is the newly-completed Islamic Centre.

219 Muzium Negara (National Museum) with part of the city in the background. This Malay-style building stands on the site of the old Selangor Museum which was bombed during the Second World War. Flanking the main entrance of the museum are two huge murals in Italian glass mosaic depicting the country's historical episodes and main cultural activities. Among others, the museum contains exhibits relating to the country's history, arts and crafts, weapons, currency, birds and mammals. Exhibits from other museums and personal collections are occasionally displayed here too. Bordering the museum are new highways built to divert traffic from the city centre.

218   219

221

220 The National Mosque in Kuala Lumpur. The main dome of the mosque is designed in the shape of an 18-point star, representing the country's 13 states and the 5 Pillars of Islam. The interior of the mosque houses, among other things, a mausoleum and a reflecting pool with a 73-metre minaret rising from it.

221 Muslims are required to pray five times a day. Friday is the official prayer day where thousands of Muslims from all over the country will gather at mosques to pray. Before they pray, they are required to wash themselves at nearby taps before entering the prayer hall.

222 *(following page)* Situated at the confluence of the Kelang and Gombak rivers is Masjid Jamek. Said to be built on the spot where Kuala Lumpur was born in 1857, this 77-year-old mosque was the city's main mosque before the National Mosque was built. It was restored in 1983 as one of the country's national heritage.

223 *(following page)* Muslims at their Friday prayers in Masjid Jamek. As the mosque is located in the heart of Kuala Lumpur, Muslims working in the city find it very convenient to conduct their prayers at this mosque which is usually packed.

220

224 The heart of the city with Jalan Kuching in the foreground. Among the newer high-rise buildings that have sprung up recently are the new extensions to Bank Negara (the country's central bank), the Chung Khiaw Bank, the Menara Tun Razak and the Employees Provident Fund (EPF) buildings in the foreground. Jalan Tuanku Abdul Rahman *(left)*, flanked by older shophouses and a few newer edifices, is one of the city's busiest thoroughfares and shopping areas. Behind the patch of greenery *(left)* is part of the Golden Triangle, the city's fastest growing area. On the right is the Royal Selangor Club field where Malaysia's National Day celebrations are usually held. Facing the field are the Sultan Abdul Samad building, formerly the State Secretariat building and now the High Courts premises, and the Royal Selangor Club, also known as the "Spotted Dog". The dome-shaped structure *(right)* is Stadium Negara, the country's main indoor stadium where many international and national sport meets are held.

225 *(following page)* A view of the city with Sungei Gombak on the left and Sungei Kelang on the right. The triangular plot of land bounded by Sungei Gombak, Jalan Dang Wangi and Jalan Munshi Abdullah is the site of the proposed "city within a city" project. Dubbed a "mini Manhattan", this mini-city project to be developed over a period of 8 to 12 years will feature three main office blocks ranging from 35 to 48 storeys, office suites, an international hotel and other modern amenities. Flanked by two blocks of white buildings in the foreground is the restored Loke building, one of the city's first brick houses. Situated on a hillock on the right are the offices of the Prime Minister's Department.

226 A band performance, one of the many highlights of National Day parades. National Day celebrations in the city are always colourful affairs with Malaysians from all walks of life including the King, the Prime Minister and Cabinet Ministers turning up in full force at the Royal Selangor Club Field, the annual venue for National Day parades.

227 Malaysian youths in exuberant mood as they cheer their home team.

228 Artillery officers of the Malay Regiment in their smart ceremonial uniform preparing their cannons for a gun salute in conjunction with the National Day celebration.

229 The Taming Sari, an aerobatic team of the Royal Malaysian Air Force (RMAF) stages aerobatic display in their PC-7 aircraft over the country's cerulean sky on auspicious occasion such as the Naitonal Day or the Armed Forces Day celebrations.

230 *(following page)* Located in one of the city's busiest areas bounded roughly by Jalan Petaling *(pictured)*, Jalan Sultan and Jalan Bandar is Chinatown where a myriad of interesting items ranging from jeans, household goods, fruits, flowers and ancient medicine to roast ducks and sweetmeat are sold. At dusk, Jalan Petaling is closed to traffic and the entire area is converted into an open-air pasar malam or night market. Under the glare of electricity and gas light, the hum of activity continues late into the night.

231, 232 *(following page)* Lanterns in various shapes, sizes and iridescent colours are sold weeks before the Moon Cake Festival, an annual event celebrated by Chinese on the fifteenth day of the Chinese eighth month (August or September). This convivial festivity celebrated in high spirit and enthusiasm has its origins in ancient China during the Mongolian invasion. The Chinese, who were under bondage for many years,

were freed after a young genius Lum Pak Woon successfully united the captives in repelling the invasion. Lum Pak Woon had on the fifteenth day of the eighth moon hidden secret messages in the moon cakes distributed to various Chinese households. In these messages were strategies planned to repudiate the Mongolians. Their success so pleased the Chinese Emperor that he made that date an auspicious day to commemorate their freedom from bondage. To this day, Chinese all over the world celebrate this festival in the traditions of their ancestors — with the eating of moon cakes, a delicacy made of pastry and lotus seed paste and the lighting of lanterns. In many homes, food such as moon cakes, sweetmeat and chicken are offered to the Moon Goddess.

233 In a fast-moving metropolis like Kuala Lumpur where the younger generation is very much influenced by western culture, Chinese street opera is still being perpetuated. This dramatic musical performance, believed to have started during the Sung Dynasty (960-1279 A.D.) in China, features actors and actresses with heavy make-up dressed in resplendent costumes. Usually performed on special stages in front of temples and in open space in predominantly Chinese areas and occasionally in shopping complexes and even hotels, Chinese street opera in a number of dialects such as Cantonese, Teochew and Hokkien draws large crowds of young and old. The plot usually revolves around common themes such as love and stories of legendary heroes and heroines and dynasty warlords. For example, the most popular Cantonese opera today, "Dai Looi Fah", depicts the tragedy of Princess Cheung Ping, the last Ming princess who committed suicide after China was taken over by the Manchurians while the "Dream of the Red Chamber" is about the tragedy of thwarted love between Pao-yu and his cousin, Black Jade.

234 Wesak Day, a triple celebration commemorating the birth, enlightenment and death of Buddha, is the most important and sacred Buddhist festival. Early in the morning, Buddhists gather at temples to pray while in the evening, certain temples hold candlelight processions of floats adorned with lights, lotus, chrysanthemums and orchids accompanying a special float carrying the statue of Buddha.

235 *(previous page)* Lion dances are usually performed during Chinese New Year, the opening of new businesses and other festive occasions to drive away the evil so that only good luck and prosperity remain.

236, 237 Thaipusam, the birthday of the Hindu deity, Lord Subramaniam, is one of the most important festivals of Malaysian Hindus. Usually held in late January or early February, this religious festival is celebrated in major Hindu temples throughout the country but the most spectacular celebration is held at the Batu Caves. A day before the festival, an ornate chariot containing the statue of Lord Subramaniam drawn by two garlanded bulls is escorted by thousands of Hindu devotees to the Batu Caves. On the day of the festival, hundreds of thousands of devotees gather at the Batu Caves grounds to seek penance for past misdeeds and to fulfill vows made during the year. The highlight of this festival is undoubtedly the thousands of devotees carrying resplendent *kavadis* (wooden religious structures adorned with flowers, peacock feathers and fruits). Many of them have long skewers, spikes and other sharp implements pierced through their tongues, cheeks and bodies. The devotees are required to carry their kavadis up the 272 steps to the Sri Subramaniam (Sri Murugan) Temple housing the statue of Lord Subramaniam. As they journey up the steps, fellow devotees sing religious songs and shout "vel! vel!" accompanied by *tablas* (Indian drums). At the temple, the burdens of the *kavadi*-bearers are removed by priests. The devotees also bring offerings of coconuts, milk and fruits to Lord Subramaniam. Parents bring along their babies to have their heads shaven to procure their future well-being.

238 A Hindu wedding is a colourful, gay and joyful occasion. Great importance is placed on the setting of the wedding date because it is believed that it will affect the future of the new couple. After a detailed study of the horoscopes of the bride and groom, a Hindu priest provides the families of the bride and groom with a few sets of wedding date and time. Once the date and time are decided by the two families, preparations for the wedding begin. The wedding ceremony is conducted by a priest in the presence of family members, relatives and friends either at the home of the bride or groom, a temple or a community hall. This is followed by a grand feast.

239 A traditional Malay marriage is an elaborate affair involving numerous ceremonies. The whole process begins with the *merisek* (making quiet enquiries) where the groom's close relatives, usually his uncle or aunt, visit the home of a close relative of the prospective bride to make the necessary enquiries such as the "availability" of the girl and her background. Later, representatives of the groom go to the prospective bride's home for the *meminang* ceremony to ask for the girl's hand in marriage. This is followed by the *bertunang* (engagement) ceremony. Finally, on the wedding day, the couple goes through the *akad nikah* (marriage contract) ceremony which is usually held in the morning. Later in the day, which is usually in the afternoon, the *bersanding* (tying the nuptial knots) is held. The bride and groom sit side by side on a colourful dais to receive blessings from relatives and friends. Like in other weddings, a big feast attended by family, relatives and friends is held after the *bersanding* ceremony.

240 242
241

240, 241, 242 Eating out is a recognized pastime for many Malaysians. The city abounds with numerous fast-food outlets, restaurants and open-air stalls, serving a seemingly endless array of food from Kentucky Fried Chicken or Wendy's Burgers to a potpourri of Chinese, Malay and Indian specialities. For hawkers' specialities, there are scores of open-air stalls in street corners or open-air squares in Jalan Imbi, Jalan Pasar and Jalan Chow Kit. These stalls serve a wide variety of food such as Hokkien fried mee, a tasty noodle dish fried with meat, vegetables and black sauce *(242)*, *satay* (morsels of beef, chicken or lamb) barbequed over an open coal fire and eaten with spicy peanut-chilli sauce *(241)*, and *roti canai*, Indian bread served with either fish or meat curry or the famous Indian *dhall* *(240)*.

243 *(following page)* St Mary's Church, standing forlorn beside its more illustrious neighbour, the Royal Selangor Club, is one of Kuala Lumpur's oldest churches. The original church, located on a hill now known as Bukit Aman, was a wooden building erected in 1886. This permanent brick building based on the early Gothic architecture style was built in 1894.

244 *(following page)* A worship service at Calvary Church, one of Kuala Lumpur's leading churches. The church is located in a quiet residential area of Damansara Heights.

245 Kenny Hills, Kuala Lumpur's own Sunset Boulevard. This elite residential area provides comfortable living environment for the city's *nouveau riche*.

246 *(following page)* Kuala Lumpur's commercial boom has also brought about a corresponding population explosion too as more and more people from the countryside migrate to the city in search of better economic opportunities. To accommodate this growing population, housing estates such as this in Bangsar are mushrooming throughout the city. Most of these housing estates have shops, mini-markets, restaurants and coffee shops while the bigger ones even have banks, post offices, shopping complexes, offices and cinemas.

247 249
248

247 The Tunku Abdul Rahman Hall in Jalan Ampang has a colourful historic past. The first Parliament sitting in 1959 was held here before the Parliament House was built. This stately building was also the venue for the installation of two Yang di-Pertuan Agong, the country's Supreme Head of State, and the declaration of Kuala Lumpur as a city in 1972. The National Art Gallery was housed here before it was shifted to the Majestic Hotel building opposite the Central Railway Station.

248 The old City Hall building, now maintained as a historic relic, was among the earliest major buildings to be erected in Kuala Lumpur. Built between 1894 and 1897, this Moorish-style building is based on the same general design as the Sultan Abdul Samad building, another historic building along the same road.

249 *(previous page)* Located beside Jalan Tun Abdul Razak is the Royal Selangor Golf Club, one of the oldest golf clubs in this region. Established in 1893, the golf club was converted into an arms school while its land was used for cultivating tapioca, bananas and vegetables during the Japanese occupation of the country. Today, the club has about 2,500 members who include royalty, politicians and heads of corporations. Among its facilities are a 36-hole golf course, indoor and outdoor tennis courts, billiards and snooker rooms, squash courts and two swimming pools.

250 Government administrative complexes in Jalan Duta on the outskirts of the city. Behind the complexes are the city's lower courts buildings. Over the years, the Government has shifted a number of its offices to the outskirts to decentralize traffic within the city centre. Public sector's working hours are slightly different from those in the private sector. Thus, the city has two sets of peak hours, one for the public sector and another for the private sector. This is partly aimed at easing traffic congestion within the city. In the foreground is the National Archives Building.

251 The Tun Razak Hockey Stadium, the country's first astroturf stadium, is situated beside Jalan Duta. Named after the country's second Prime Minister, the late Tun Abdul Razak, this multi-million stadium has been the venue for many hockey tournaments both at national and international levels since its opening in 1982. A proposed sports complex with squash, netball, volleyball and sepak takraw facilities will soon be built here.

252 The Putra World Trade Centre, South-East Asia's premier convention centre. Named after Malaysia's first Prime Minister, Tunku Abdul Rahman Putra Al-Haj, this ultra-modern integrated business facility comprises the 41-storey Menara Datuk Onn tower block, the Dewan Merdeka, a plenary hall which can seat 3,500 people, the Dewan Tun Razak exhibition centre, two large conference halls known as Dewan Tun Hussein and Dewan Tun Ismail, 13 meeting rooms, meeting areas, shopping arcade, restaurants, bank and guest lounges. The centre, which also houses the headquarters of the United Malay National Organization (UMNO), the largest component party in the ruling Coalition Government, has a wide range of sophisticated facilities for conventions, exhibitions and other functions. Its first major convention will be the Pata conference in April 1986. Located next to the Putra World Trade Centre is the 600-room Pan-Pacific Hotel.

253 *(following page)* Jalan Sultan Ismail, the city's hotel belt where modish hotels like the Merlin, Equatorial, Hilton and Shangri-La are located. Also situated here are other modern high-rise buildings housing the headquarters of big corporations such as the Malaysian Airline System (MAS), Promet and ESSO.